TRADING FUTURES

A BEGINNER'S GUIDE

TRADEX

Founder, Red Pill Trading

This book is dedicated to traders globally, new and old, who have a thirst for knowledge and growth.

Copyright © 2024 Trade X, Red Pill Trading.

All Rights Reserved.

No part of this publication may be reproduced, stored in a retrieval system, or transmitted in any form or by any means, electronic, mechanical, photocopying or otherwise, without written permission of the author.

Disclaimer: No part of this book should be constituted as financial advice. Always seek the guidance of a certified financial advisor before placing capital (money) into the markets.

Set in 10/12 pt Poppins

Illustrations: By Sketchify
Editor: Pavel Stanishev
Author: TradeX

www.redpill-trading.com

Printed in the United Kingdom

TABLE OF CONTENTS

INTRODUCTION 7

FUTURES TERMINOLOGY 23

    MARGIN 23

    MAINTENANCE MARGIN 25

    MARGIN CALL 27

    SETTLEMENT DAY 28

    STANDARDISATION 28

FUTURES MARKET 31

    PHYSICAL FUTURES 33

    FINANCIAL FUTURES 34

WHERE ARE FUTURES TRADED? 37

FUTURES IN A NUTSHELL 41

INDEX FUTURES – A BRIEF LOOK 45

FUTURES ASSET CLASSES 51

    CURRENCIES 53

- ENERGY 63
- FINANCIALS 77
- METALS 87
- GRAINS 97
- MEATS 103
- SOFTS 107
- INDICES 115
- E-MINI AND MICRO CONTRACTS 127
- THE WORLD OF PROPRIETARY FIRMS 137
- FINAL WORDS 145
- GLOSSARY 149
- ACKNOWLEDGMENTS 171
- SOURCES 173
- NOTES 175

For my better half Rebecca,
Thank you for an incredible 16 years.
Here's to the next 16 and beyond.

Why did I write this book?

Let's start with a simple quote:

> ***Mountains can't be moved,***
> ***they can only be climbed.***
> ***It all starts with taking***
> ***that first step.***

INTRODUCTION

Often, we as humans, make excuses or reasons for why we can't do something. It's the now infamous old chimp from The Chimp Paradox by Professor Steve Peters that resides in our psyche that seeks out comfort and security. A blanket protecting us from the cold of failure. There is nothing wrong with that until, of course, you reach the inevitable wall, the state of burnout, fatigue, and exhaustion of a life being lived purely by means of existence where things get tricky. I know because I have been there in my 20s working the treadmill office job. But for those who do finally decide to take a risk on themselves and trust life's course, which undoubtedly will be set full of roadblocks as a test of one's resolve on route to life's true Dharma, well, that's where things get less tricky and slightly more interesting.

For those who have considered, dreamt, or maybe flirted with the idea of trading over the years and thought, could I be a Trader? Well, let me tell you, today, in this modern age, there is no better time to take that leap of faith.

This book aims to serve as the initial first step for anyone seeking to climb their own trading mountain, regardless of experience or background, starting their journey, or simply wanting to further their knowledge in the Futures Markets. So, let's get straight to it.

My primary goal is to demystify the world of financial instruments, focusing specifically on the Futures market and the asset classes within. I understand that the terminology, acronyms, and complexities of trading can feel like learning a new language, overwhelming at times. That's why I aim to simplify the concepts, making them easy to navigate and understand. I won't delve into unnecessary minutiae or overly complex topics that aren't essential for trading futures. Instead, my focus will be on providing fundamental knowledge across asset classes to empower you to make informed decisions about whether trading futures is right for you. I'll explain what futures are and how to trade them, provide examples of how they work in practice, deliver a glossary of terminology while also offering guidance on possibly starting your own journey with minimal capital, through proprietary firms, which are still operational as of writing. At the back of the book, you'll find a glossary in case there are words or phrases you may not be familiar with. Revert to this at any stage whilst reading this book or, of course, at any time in the future. My ultimate goal is to provide a valuable resource for traders considering entering the world of futures trading, equipping them with the insights they need to take that leap with greater confidence and minimal friction. This book is ideal for anyone new to futures or who has experienced the market firsthand but is seeking a deeper understanding of the sector.

Now, if you've come across this book, chances are you're already familiar with me as Trade_X. Whether you've seen my live trading sessions on YouTube under the same name or encountered me through my private trading community, Red Pill Trading, the company I founded in late 2023, either way, I'm blessed to connect with you.

Education on how to trade is the cornerstone of everything we do, so much so that we've established a university where we break down my trading strategies in a top-down, easy-to-follow, detailed learning environment. It's here where you'll find me trading futures live every day from

4 am UTC to 4 pm UTC, Monday to Friday, providing members with real-time insights and opportunities.

However, this environment is for those who already have a basic understanding of Futures Trading and are looking to take their trading to the next level, so it got me thinking. How else can I help those who have limited or, no knowledge at all?

The answer, I hope, is in this book, which has emerged from the aspiration to offer an understanding of the fundamentals of the financial futures markets to those already equipped with a basic comprehension of trading.

But before we delve into the intricacies of trading futures, allow me a moment to share a short snapshot of my journey to date.

Why I'm sharing my journey with you in brief is to provide insight into my motivations and decisions, particularly in transitioning towards trading futures. Understanding the journey that led me here may resonate with you if you're considering a similar path or exploring new trading opportunities. Perhaps you, too, have been searching for an optimal trading environment but haven't quite found it yet. By sharing my experiences, I hope to offer you a roadmap of sorts—a guiding light as you navigate your own trading journey. Whether you're intrigued by the potential of futures trading or simply seeking a new approach, I hope my journey will resonate with you and provide valuable insights as you chart your course in the world of finance.

So, it's been a rewarding path for sure, shaped of course by both success and failures. This inevitable caldron of different experiences has without doubt contributed to my overall understanding and appreciation of the market. Something today in hindsight I wouldn't change for the world, but at the time would have changed in a heartbeat!

That being said, like most traders I'm sure, it's been a meander through different styles and approaches that has ultimately led me to where I am now and shaped me into the trader I've become.

In the interest of brevity, I'll forego discussing my other business ventures for this book, perhaps saving that for a future publication. So with that in mind, let's start with what really matters here, the beginning of my trading journey.

It all started in 2016 when I utilised funds from another business endeavour to embark on this new venture. Initially, of course, my experience in the field was limited, so I followed the traditional route; depositing funds into a financial services company, in my case, Hargreaves Lansdown in the UK, and began long-term positional trading, buying, and selling shares primarily in Blue Chip and Tech sectors.

As expected for someone relatively new to trading, I experienced both gains and losses. Nothing new here, ey! Although spinning on this proverbial hamster wheel, what became immediately apparent however was the immense potential for both financial gain and losses within the markets. In the same way a hamster or gerbil will always return to the wheel, I kept returning to the charts. They had me hooked, and it was decided right there and then that I was going to become a trader no matter what happens - No plan B. Just like the mouse churning milk into cream so he could escape the bucket and survive, all I had to do was find my method for success and escaping the now infamous 'life Matrix'.

Despite realising the potential trading had to offer by witnessing it first hand, I never aspired to become a Warren Buffet-type investor, meticulously analysing each and every aspect of a company, from its debt-to-equity ratios to quarterly statements, holding for extended periods of time in the hope your predictions are correct. What works for one doesn't necessarily work for another, right, and let's not forget Warren Buffet can look into the whites of the eyes of Board Members before cementing a position. For the lowly speculative investor however, that's a tad farfetched. While undoubtedly his style is effective, such an approach didn't align with my personality or lifestyle.

So, in my 30s, with a penchant for understanding every detail and with a combined thirst and desire for immediate feedback on my actions, I sought a trading style that offered more control and provided immediate results. Whether investing in a business or playing a round of golf, I prefer knowing the outcome of my actions right away. Metaphorically, if I hit a golf ball and it fades into the trees, it clearly signals that something in my swing went wrong. This prompts me to immediately assess what went awry and seek answers on how to correct it, intent on preventing making that same mistake again. Questionable metaphor - I agree, but the principles remain.

Without this instant feedback, the feeling of being unsettled is strong. Striving for continuous improvement and refinement in every single aspect has become something of an addiction and character trait. Maybe this has something to do with being blessed / cursed with an overly active mind! Who knows, but I new I had to be active in the charts.

I therefore begun the quest of seeking a more active approach, one where I could manage the positions regularly and where immediate feedback was provided. After researching potential sectors to day trade, I found myself drawn to trading small-cap stocks intraday. For those familiar with this niche of the market, I can almost see you grimacing as you read this, and to some extent, you'd be justified. Trading small-caps stocks provided me with everything I craved and then some: immediate feedback, volatile conditions, and an undeniable allure of financial gain. However, it also came with a sobering reality check – the potential for significant financial loss loomed just as large.

Undeterred and steadfast on trading becoming a new career, over the course of two years, I immersed myself in the world of small caps, soaking up knowledge about the fundamental operations of the marketplace, delving into the intricacies of brokers, some offering direct market access whilst others operated differently, level II data as well as the mysterious realms of dark pools and institutional investment funds. This period marked the steepest learning curve of my trading journey and provided invaluable insights on how money truly moves.

As a side note, despite the risks and challenges inherent in trading small-cap stocks, I still believe there's immense value in experiencing this realm for any new trader. If you want to grasp the principles of volatility first-hand, there's no better classroom than observing a small-cap stock skyrocketing on the back of a positive news release. It's a visceral lesson that leaves an indelible mark on your understanding of the markets.

Nevertheless, for those who have traded small caps, the depth of research required for each trade remains abundantly clear. Even within this volatile arena, a systematic approach was crucial, and that's precisely what I employed, focusing solely on small market capitalisation stocks that exhibited continuation after significant price gaps in anticipation of news releases. My strategy centred on trading breakouts, capitalising on small price ranges by entering positions on pullbacks shortly after a news-driven surge.

However, here's the catch: while trading this model during a bull market can feel like cruising in a Rolls Royce, navigating through a bear market is more akin to driving a Morris Minor in terms of comfort. Those breakouts don't stay breakouts for long! Anyhow, this profitable yet challenging journey provided me with a profound understanding of market manipulation. Manipulation in terms of the way price is delivered vs manipulation in a cynical sense. It's not an exaggeration to claim that the small-cap stocks sector is among the most aggressively manipulated sectors in the market with regards to price delivery.

In the world of small caps, market movements are often orchestrated to coincide with the release of specific words or phrases within news releases. For instance, manipulation here is when the announcement of positive earnings triggers an immediate expansion in price one direction, which ultimately moves opposite to the eventual trend. My eyes were truly opened, and the desire to learn exactly how to trade in sync with that manipulation became my primary goal.

In my quest for seeking a perfect trading environment and for clarity, in my eyes, that revolved around being active - day trading, required minimal fundamental analysis, therefore technical, and was framed around precise entries and exits centred around manipulation. I found myself in late 2019 delving into options trading as a new approach after becoming disillusioned with small caps, concentrating on the S&P 500 and Nasdaq 100. These indices, the Nasdaq Composite and the S&P 500 are benchmarks for the US stock market. Although there's a third index, the Dow Jones, which I'll touch on later, I initially focused on the top 10 Blue Chip and Tech Stocks within these indexes. Yet, as time progressed, I expanded my scope to include the indexes themselves. This led me to discover the opportunity to trade the actual index rather than individual companies inside the index, facilitated by options contracts tied to ETFs like SPY and QQQ. These derivatives grant holders the right to buy or sell a specified number of shares of the underlying asset at a predetermined price within a set timeframe. Without wanting to dive too far away from futures, what was important and intrigued me about this approach was the reduction in analysis. So, instead of monitoring numerous individual stocks, I could now fully concentrate on trading the indexes themselves via ETF derivatives. It felt like I was finally finding my home. This shift provided the volatility I sought in derivative contracts by using leverage (discussed later), but it also streamlined my trading strategy to focus solely on two indexes. With less emphasis on individual stock movements and more on the fundamental state of the market, I found a more refined and focused approach to my trading strategy.

However, what was still missing was the real understanding of price delivery from a mechanical viewpoint. I had strategies, but there were always questions. This all changed when after delving into ICT in late 2019, I fell into ICT's orbit fully in early 2020, and suddenly, everything began clicking into place. All the puzzle pieces of my trading journey fell neatly together. I started to comprehend the fundamental principles of how price behaves and gained insights into market dynamics, market manipulation, and the significance of various markets and their interconnectedness, all focused around the futures market. Now futures contracts, like options contracts, are derivative contracts, we'll go through this in detail throughout the book. But by switching to futures, it enabled me to remove the additional levels of complexity that came with Option contracts, such as the Greeks. Here, while trading futures, I began creating my own strategies using the information gained and developed my own set of rules and protocols, developing new protocols which aren't taught anywhere else on the world wide web! These protocols and strategies still form the backbone of my trading today and is something I'm proud to say I now pay forward by teaching others to do the same.

Now, before we get into the nuts and bolts of this book, which I'm guessing by now is what you want to hear, is what truly tied it all together, and that was grasping how 21st-century markets are delivered. This understanding of price delivery brought forth a new level of clarity and precision, unlocking the final piece I'd been relentlessly seeking since embarking on my trading journey over six years ago – Getting coordinated with manipulation.

I'd finally arrived, I now had a strategy and approach defined and distilled down to incredibly precise mechanical entries, focused funnily enough, around manipulation in a sector that allowed me to streamline the process of entering and exiting trades via the futures markets whilst doing this actively by intra-day trading. To this day I still find it odd how manipulation which once baffled, now forms the cornerstone of how I trade. Hallelujah! Life works in mysterious ways, huh! With that, futures trading had become my home.

INTRODUCTION

TRADING FUTURES

FUTURES TERMINOLOGY

So, let's start with some important aspects you need to consider before placing any futures trade. Note: this is applicable if you're trading with personal funds. If you're trading with proprietary firms, which is discussed later, many of these do not apply. However, if you intend to deploy capital directly into the markets, pay close attention.

MARGIN

Futures margin refers to the essential funds held in a brokerage account that safeguard both the trader and the broker against potential losses in an open trade. Without sufficient margin in your brokerage account, you cannot trade. Typically, it constitutes a smaller fraction of the contract value, ranging from 3% to 12% of the notional futures contract value. The notional value being the total value of the underlying contract. If you're unsure of your margin requirements, you can find these via your chosen brokerage. You also need to be aware there are two categories of futures margins:

a) Intraday Margin

This is the minimum account balance mandated by the broker to maintain a position of one contract (either long or short) during trading hours. It's also known as day trading margin. Often, this will be the amount you need to trade during RTH (Regular Trading Hours). Although ETH (Electronic Trading Hours) are available with Trading Futures, you will need enough capital to cover the Initial Margin. Again, if you are unsure of these amounts, you can check with your broker.

b) Initial Margin

This represents the per-contract minimum amount stipulated by the exchange, which must be upheld in the account to retain a position overnight. Often referred to as overnight margin, it ensures sufficient funds are available to cover potential overnight price movements.

With this deposit, or margin, futures traders can gain access to the relevant futures contract and trade instruments with a much greater value than the margin price. This difference between the margin requirement and the contracts price is known as leverage, something we'll cover later with examples. But for now, just grasp that margin is essentially a good faith payment made by you to your broker that allows you to trade futures contracts that have a much greater notional value than the margin deposited.

MAINTENANCE MARGIN

Excess margin, also referred to as maintenance margin, refers to the surplus equity in a brokerage account beyond the minimum margin requirements that the brokerage often sets. Now, let's be clear, effectively managing excess margin is crucial in futures trading to avoid potential liquidation and penalties imposed by your broker. It's the buffer in case price moves against your position, which would result in a margin call or liquidation. Liquidation, also known as offsetting, occurs when a long or short futures position is closed out by your broker due to insufficient intraday margin. So, it can't be stressed highly enough that it is essential to maintain adequate margin levels to prevent this outcome.

Trading at full leverage means utilising all available margin without any excess. This leaves absolutely no room for error, and even a minor adverse price movement could trigger forced liquidation by the trade desk or the inevitable request for a margin call. It's, therefore, always wise to hold more Intraday Margin than required to avoid this mishap. Accounts in debit, essentially violating margin requirements, are subject to liquidation in most scenarios, and you need to be aware it's not the broker's responsibility to manage your margin. They may liquidate either partially or fully without warning without ever contacting you. You've been warned.

By simply reviewing your broker's terms before depositing funds, you will see the different intraday, initial, and maintenance margins required to trade any futures contract. I've shown an example from Ninja Trader below:

Symbol	Market	Exchange	Group	Day	Initial
CC	Cocoa	ICE Futures US	Softs	$1000.00	$15422.00
CT	Cotton	ICE Futures US	Softs	$1000.00	$3300.00
KC	Coffee	ICE Futures US	Softs	$1000.00	$6600.00
LBR	Lumber	CME	Softs	$1000.00	$990.00
LBS	Random Length Lumber	CME	Softs	$1000.00	$5940.00
OJ	Orange Juice	ICE Futures US	Softs	$1000.00	$5069.00
SB	Sugar No. 11	ICE Futures US	Softs	$1000.00	$777.00
M2K	Micro E-mini Russell 2000	CME	Micro Indices	$50.00	$715.00
MES	Micro E-mini S&P 500	CME	Micro Indices	$50.00	$1226.00
MMC	Micro E-mini S&P MidCap 400 Index	CME	Micro Indices	$10.00	$1661.00
MNQ	Micro E-mini NASDAQ 100	CME	Micro Indices	$100.00	$1847.00
MSC	Micro E-mini S&P SmallCap 600 Index	CME	Micro Indices	$50.00	$1034.00
MYM	Micro E-mini Dow $0.50	CBOT	Micro Indices	$50.00	$924.00
GC	Gold	COMEX	Metals	$1000.00	$11000.00
HG	Copper	COMEX	Metals	$2476.00	$4950.00
MGC	E-Micro Gold	COMEX	Metals	$200.00	$1100.00
MHG	Micro Copper	COMEX	Metals	$300.00	$495.00
PA	Palladium	NYMEX	Metals	$2000.00	$10250.00
PL	Platinum	NYMEX	Metals	$2000.00	$2750.00
QC	E-Mini Copper	COMEX	Metals	$600.00	$2475.00

Credit, NinjaTrader; ninjatrader/pricing/margins/

MARGIN CALL

Not what you ever want to receive, let's be honest. A margin call is a notification issued by the broker to a trader when their maintenance margin falls below a certain threshold deemed safe. Upon receiving a margin call, you, the trader, are required to deposit additional funds into your account to bolster the margin and prevent your futures contracts from being automatically liquidated, potentially incurring penalties. As mentioned earlier, it should be noted that brokers may not always issue margin calls, placing the responsibility on the trader to monitor their account and ensure adequate margin levels are maintained at all times. In Layman's terms, know your margin requirements, maintain a buffer, and try your upmost best not to go below them.

To conclude this section on margins, the most straightforward approach to managing excess margin is to trade contract sizes commensurate with predetermined risk levels and account sizes, which ensures that a sufficient margin is maintained. This approach reduces liquidation risk and promotes solid risk management. Latter being paramount. As traders, our primary goal is to manage risk, so consider yourself a risk manager, not a trader!

SETTLEMENT DAY

Settlement day in futures marks the culmination of a futures contract, where all obligations are finalised. It's the designated date for the ultimate exchange of funds and, if applicable, the physical delivery of the underlying asset between the contract's buyer and seller.

STANDARDISATION

Understanding standardisation is essential to getting to grips with the fundamentals of Futures. If this doesn't make sense right now, I hope by the end of this book, it will! But for simplicity, the majority of futures contracts are standardised, meaning they are essentially interchangeable and specify specific criteria, such as:

- Quality and quantity of the commodity
- Pricing per unit of the asset and the minimum price fluctuation (tick size)

What this means is each futures contract has a certain set of specifications that make it uniform, which in turn provides a base level that anyone, whether they are an institution or a singular investor, can engage on those same terms. Ultimately providing liquidity to the marketplace. Simplifying it even further, each futures contract provides a set of specifications, the most notable for me, as the speculative investor, is the multiple of the underlying asset that a trader can leverage. We'll go into Multiples throughout this book.

***Everything is created twice.
First in the mind, and then in reality.***

– ROBIN SHARMA

FUTURES MARKET

Okay, so firstly, from a technical perspective, or better put, from a commercial or institutional investment viewpoint, so that you can understand why they exist. A futures market serves as an exchange where producers or consumers can engage in buying and selling futures contracts to hedge positions and or mitigate risks within their businesses.

From a retail or speculative trader's viewpoint, futures markets allow a trader to speculate on the underlying assets appreciation or depreciation without any intent of ever taking delivery. They're simply looking to gain from the leveraged exposure the contract provides.

I'll show examples and explain these differences inside each asset class as we go. But for now, simply understand there are those who seek to use Futures contracts in a commercial sense, and then there are those who're simply looking to gain from the movements in the contract itself by correctly predicting the direction of the underlying asset.

Next element to understand are categories, as there are categories to be aware of when it comes to the Futures Market. Let's begin opening the Chinese dolls. At the head of the family tree there are two; Physical and Non Physical, latter more commonly known as Financial Futures. To explain the difference let us consider an example from a commercial viewpoint. In a physical futures contract, such as commodities, one party commits to purchasing a specified quantity of securities or commodities, i.e., Bushels of Wheat, and agrees to take delivery on a predetermined date, while the counterparty agrees to provide the asset. Non Physical futures on the other hand, don't require delivery of a commodity and are instead cash-settled. Index Futures being a primary example. These contracts don't require physical delivery at all. What's important to know at this stage is these two categories, where one requires the provision or receiving of the underlying asset and the other, where the contract is cash-settled upon settlement, are known as Physical Futures & Financial Futures.

Investors can choose from numerous futures contracts, but each of them fall into one of those two head categories. But let's be clear for a moment because your head maybe spinning, you do not need to take delivery on either physical or financial futures as a speculator; this section is merely revealing to you the different categories and sub-categories to give you a lay of the land. Inside Physical Futures and Non-Physical futures (Financial futures), we have subcategories. We will begin by looking at the former.

PHYSICAL FUTURES

Physical futures entail the actual delivery of assets upon the contract's expiration, commonly known as the settlement date. For instance, farmers who purchase crop futures will receive the specified quantity of crops at the conclusion of the contract. Another example is crude oil, a widely traded physical future where each contract represents 1,000 barrels of crude oil. An oil producer, for example, may wish to lock in prices in the future by selling a futures contract.

Now, as mentioned, the Futures Market is similar to a set of Chinese dolls, a category inside a category, so inside physical futures, we have two subgroups; these are known as soft and hard commodities.

Soft commodities encompass an array of agricultural products, ranging from coffee and cocoa to grains like corn and wheat, as well as livestock such as lean hogs and feeder cattle. These commodities undergo a growth cycle that culminates in harvesting, typically followed by further processing. In contrast, hard commodities, including mined metals such as copper, gold, and silver, along with energy resources like crude oil and natural gas, are sourced from geological deposits. Unlike their soft counterparts, hard commodities are not cultivated but rather extracted from the earth. It's worth adding that while hard commodities exhibit global consistency in deposits, the growth of soft commodities is intrinsically tied to regional climate conditions. This difference in how they are cultivated or extracted goes a long way in providing the distinction between the two.

FINANCIAL FUTURES

Financial futures predominantly revolve around equities and other securities where physical delivery isn't necessary. With financial futures contracts, you receive assets such as stocks, Treasury bills, certificates of deposit (CDs), and other financial instruments upon contract expiration. This non-physical delivery aspect distinguishes financial futures from physical futures. Index Futures, which I'm sure you're most excited to learn about, fall into this category. This overriding category, distinguishing physical and non-physical, is not to be mixed up with Financial Futures as an asset class. Refer to the Glossary for definition distinction or review the Financial Futures Asset Class later in the book. So now we have the categories out the way, let's consider where they are traded.

TRADING FUTURES

WHERE ARE FUTURES TRADED?

Accessing futures markets requires participation in specific exchanges dedicated to futures trading. Although there are many, one prominent market is the Chicago Mercantile Exchange (CME), a cornerstone of the CME Group. CME has evolved into a global hub for derivatives trading, serving traders worldwide. Many brokerage firms that provide futures trading services are linked to this exchange, offering traders access to US markets through CME. Today, the CME Group is the world's largest futures exchange and still offers trading in a broad range of futures and options contracts across asset classes, including agricultural commodities, energy, metals, equity indexes, and foreign exchange (all discussed later). The exchange was founded in 1898 and is headquartered in Chicago, Illinois and now operates several subsidiaries, such as the Chicago Board of Trade (CBOT), the New York Mercantile Exchange (NYMEX), and the Commodity Exchange, Inc.

(COMEX). The CME Group is well known for its liquid markets and reliable price delivery. For this reason, when choosing a broker, I'd advise choosing one connected to the CME group, which, to be honest, most are, and opting for their data packages in order to trade.

Of course, there are many brokers to choose from who have access to CME should you decide to trade with personal funds. Two that I recommend are Ninja Trader - if you have an account size less than $1000 of personal capital to deploy directly into the markets as they have some very competitive margins, and commissions, along with IBKR (Interactive Brokers) if you have a larger account and can cover the cost of an individual contract (s) and want to be able to trade a diverse array of financial instruments such as stocks, options and derivate futures contracts. To be completely transparent, although I use both of these brokers today, I'm not affiliated with them, so what's expressed here is merely an opinion. Therefore, I'd always suggest doing your due diligence before depositing funds into any broker or proprietary firm.

Should you, however, have limited personal capital to deploy or simply want to look at an alternative way to access the markets, you may want to consider proprietary firms. Topstep is a primary example, a firm we will touch on a little later.

**ANYONE WHO HAS NEVER MADE
A MISTAKE HAS NEVER TRIED
ANYTHING NEW.**

– ALBERT EINSTEIN.

FUTURES IN A NUTSHELL

Now, don't be alarmed if this initially seems a tad far-fetched and mind-boggling, relax. You don't ever need to take physical delivery in order to trade futures as a speculator; it's simply important at this stage to understand the mechanics of why they're traded to better your understanding of the market itself. We'll look at how they might be traded from a speculative trader's viewpoint as we move through the book.

To understand the overriding principles of Futures contracts, let's look at a Physical Futures Contract - Crude Oil, from a commercial angle:

Imagine an airline company seeking to stabilise its jet fuel expenses to shield against unexpected price hikes. To achieve this, they could purchase a futures contract agreeing to buy a predetermined volume of jet fuel at a fixed price for future delivery.

On the other hand, a fuel distributor might sell a futures contract to ensure a consistent market for its product and safeguard against unanticipated price drops. Both parties are agreeing on specific terms, such as purchasing or selling 1 million gallons of fuel, with delivery scheduled in 90 days at a price of $3.42 per gallon.

Now, you might be thinking, "X, I don't run a private jet company or distribute jet fuel—yet, anyway." That's perfectly fine because, as mentioned above, not everyone participating in the futures market intends to exchange a physical product in the future.

Some of us, like myself, are futures investors or speculators. We're here just to capitalise on price fluctuations within the contracts themselves. For instance, if the price of jet fuel or the value of the S&P 500 rises, the corresponding futures contract also increases in value. Whether trading commodities or indexes, individuals like us can buy and sell futures contracts without any intention of taking delivery of the underlying commodity. Instead, we're here to leverage price movements and profit from our market predictions. To put this into perspective, my personal interest is in high impact news events such as FOMC or CPI Data that can cause market volatility and worrying about capitalising on those subsequent price movements vs worrying about locking in Jet fuel prices for future delivery in my Jet fuel distribution company! Don't know why I keep talking about jets, manifesting possibly.

Jokes aside, let's clarify something important straight off the bat: not every futures contract results in the immediate delivery of the underlying asset upon settlement. Take, for example, a contract of crude oil. If you hold onto it but don't actually want to receive 1000 barrels of crude oil on your doorstep, it'd be wise to settle or close your contract before it expires. Now, with a financial futures contract, such as Index Futures, as we now know, these are cash settled, so the balance difference is due upon contract expiration between both parties. For most day traders, like me, closing before settlement is almost an irrelevance as we are in and out of our trades in a matter of minutes or hours vs weeks or months. There are options for rolling over contracts if you happen to be holding through a contract, but this can be expensive. In some cases, such as interest rate futures, which also fall under the financial futures category discussed below, physical delivery of Bonds (Paper documents) is applicable. However, if all you want to trade is Indexes, the physical nature of delivery isn't even on the horizon as these are cash-settled on settlement. But remember, as speculators you don't need to hold to settlement! Simply capitalise on price fluctuation in both Physical and Financial Futures by correctly predicting the direction of the underlying asset.

Before we delve into the various asset classes you can trade, let's start by touching on one where you won't have to supply or receive the underlying asset on the settlement date —index futures. This is the asset class that I trade every day, so let's break it down briefly by looking at its history. We'll go into it in more detail later.

INDEX FUTURES – A BRIEF LOOK

Indices, particularly stock index futures contracts, are among the most actively traded futures by speculators, and it's by no surprise, considering stock indexes such as the Dow Jones Industrial Average, the S&P 500, and the Nasdaq Composite, along with the individual stocks they comprise, are often some of the most talked about, monitored, and reported-on financial instruments globally. You only need to turn on the News Channel at some stage in the day to find a reporter or analyst discussing the latest figures and what that could mean longer term for the overall health of the economy. Consequently, futures in this domain typically, and I stress typically, provide potential for both irregular and extreme volatility on news delivered outcomes. In general, from my own experience, Index futures offer the highest liquidity and volatility compared to the other asset classes when balanced out across the course of a year.

Partly due to too the weekly supply of high impact news events that provide the catalyst.

Interestingly, stock index futures were a relatively late addition to the futures market scene. The origins of futures trading can be traced back to grains in 1848 when a group of grain merchants established the Chicago Board of Trade (CBOT), as they sought to hedge against future price fluctuations due to unpredictable weather conditions that were affecting crop production. An incredible move given the state of the climate in today's modern age you might think! Anyway, this exchange has since been bought by the CME Group, but the introduction of the S&P 500 and Nasdaq futures contracts didn't occur until 1982. These were enormous contracts for their time and were targeted towards large institutional funds and so it wasn't until 1997, with the aim of enhancing accessibility by reducing the contract multiplier, that the E-mini line of futures was introduced, now $1/5^{th}$ the size of the original contract. Since then, Micro contracts have also emerged, which are $1/10^{th}$ the size, offering an even lower barrier to entry for traders. But let's take a pause here; we'll dive into E-Mini and Micro contracts in more detail later, so for now, park this inside your medulla!

Staying on indexes for a moment, yet highlighting an important theme running through futures, is the importance of knowing how the prices of all index futures contracts are essentially a multiple of the values of the stocks within their respective indexes. If this is your first introduction to Futures, I get it's a bit of a tongue twister, indeed reading it twice might be necessary. How we discover what those multipliers are, is by reviewing the individual Index futures specification. You can find this on your brokers platform or simply check the CME website. We'll look at how these multipliers work in practice within each asset class as we move through the book, but don't worry, it's not nearly as difficult or confusing as it may initially seem.

Keeping it surface level for the time being, unlike physical futures contracts, stock index futures contracts don't involve physical delivery. You can't actually exchange little slices of the top, most capitalised 500 stocks in the S&P 500, for example – no matter how much you may fancy half a tyre from a TESLA truck. Instead, these contracts are cash-settled, meaning that on the last day of the contract's life, the buyer and seller receive the cash difference, credited or debited, depending on the outcome of the trade. As speculators, you're simply looking to trade the volatility in the underlying asset and gain from those intraday fluctuations with no intention whatsoever of taking the contract through to settlement. Stock index futures are of course traded globally, with their underlying assets (Index's) comprising some of the most well-known entities in finance. The most notable cover the US markets and include the S&P 500, Nasdaq-100, and Dow Jones Industrial Average (DJIA). Internationally, there's the Hong Kong's Hang Seng, Japan's Nikkei, the United Kingdom's "Footsie" (FTSE), Germany's DAX, and France's CAC 40 to name but a few.

Returning to the trading journey I shared briefly earlier, my strategy centres on simplicity and precision — sticking to what works best. Consequently, I concentrate solely on the Index Futures in the NASDAQ 100 (Ticker: NQ), S&P 500 (Ticker: ES), and occasionally on metals such as Gold (Ticker: GC) and Energy futures in Crude Oil (Ticker: CL)

While we'll explore index futures in more detail later, let us shift our focus to the other available asset classes you may want to consider, starting with Currencies and working our way through. Let's get into it.

TRADING FUTURES

FUTURES ASSET CLASSES

How I've structured each asset class is as follows. Firstly, I'll share foundational information, then I'll dive into how they work and touch on what they are used for. I'll conclude each section with a worked example aiding in your understanding of the mechanics on how to trade them.

> *In the rear of this book, you'll discover several pages designated for your own personal notes. If you're anything like me, jotting things down is key to solidifying it in your memory. Review each section and record the aspects that resonate with you. Consider jotting down hypothetical profit/loss scenarios for trades in the asset classes you're interested in. Enjoy the process and explore how much money could be gained, or lost! This step will help in mastering the standardisation and multiplayer combinations across asset classes.*

Trading Trifecta

CURRENCIES

Currencies are traded on the Chicago Mercantile Exchange for 23 hours a day, starting from 5:00 pm Central Time and running through to 4:00 pm Central Time the following day. Much like any other futures contract this is done via electronic Trading hours (ETH). However, the volatility of each currency contract varies depending on the time of day, aligned with the opening hours of their respective country's markets. For instance, trading the Japanese Yen may experience heightened volatility when the JPX (Japanese Exchange) opens. It's always wise to be aware of when the stock market opens in the respective countries of the currency you're looking to trade.

Currency futures contracts, also known as foreign exchange futures (FX futures), involve exchanging one currency for another at a fixed exchange rate on a specified future date. Each currency futures contract represents a specific amount of the base currency in the pair, quoted in terms of the counter currency. For example, if the price of a EUR/USD currency futures contract is 1.1100, it means that 1 euro is equivalent to 1.1100 US dollars. In layman's, 1 euro in exchange for 1.11 US Dollars.

Here's the juicy part, the size of a currency futures contract denotes the standardised volume of the base currency within the contract. Come again?! Hang in there. For instance, the typical EUR/USD currency futures contract generally represents 125,000 euros. While standardisation varies across asset classes, in the case of Currency Futures, it usually has contract sizes of 125,000. Examples of how this works in practice are shown below if you're still struggling with the concept.

It's worth noting there may also be E-mini and Micro currency futures contracts offered for the pair you're looking to trade, featuring smaller contract sizes tailored to accommodate traders and investors with reduced capital. To find these details, review your broker's Currency Futures Tab and look for the available Contracts to Trade. We'll go into E-Mini and Micro contracts later in the book, but to find them, simply look for E-Mini or Micro in the contracts title.

Since the value of these contracts is derived from the underlying currency exchange rate, currency futures are classified as financial derivatives and, as per the norm, are traded on centralised exchanges, adding to their accessibility and liquidity.

HOW DO CURRENCY FUTURES WORK?

Currency futures, like all futures contracts, work through standardised contracts, traded on centralised exchanges and, as mentioned, can be either cash-settled or physically delivered. Cash-settled contracts are settled daily and are based on mark-to-market pricing, meaning the differences are settled in cash until the expiration date. On the other hand, physically delivered contracts require the actual exchange of currencies at the expiration date in accordance with the contract size. There are a number of key elements to any futures contract, and these elements are principles running throughout the Futures Market, so let's take a dive into those using Currency Futures as an example.

Foreign exchange futures contracts key components:

- **Underlying Asset**: This refers to the specified currency exchange rate.
- **Expiration Date**: For cash-settled futures, this marks the final settlement date, while for physically delivered futures, it's the date when the currencies are exchanged. As speculators, you're simply looking to trade cash-settled contracts intra-day.

- **Contract Standardisation**: Contract sizes are standardised, such as 125,000 euros for a euro currency contract. We'll look at a trade example below.
- **Tick Change**: Refers to the minimum price movement related to each incremental change. (Tick movement) Refer to Glossary for in depth overview.
- **Margin Requirement**: Like all futures contracts, an initial margin is needed to enter into a futures contract. A maintenance margin is also established. And, of course, if the initial margin falls below this level, a margin call will occur.

WHAT ARE CURRENCY FUTURES USED FOR?

In real terms, i.e., for non-speculative traders, Currency futures serve multiple purposes, such as hedging against currency risk and speculation on future exchange rate movements. Here are some examples of how they might be used:

1. **Hedging**: Companies or individuals who anticipate needing foreign currency in the future but want to protect against potential exchange rate fluctuations can use currency futures to establish a fixed exchange rate. By buying currency futures contracts, they lock

in a rate, ensuring they won't be negatively impacted by unfavourable exchange rate movements when they need to make the currency exchange.

2. Cash Flow Management: Businesses with future cash flows in foreign currencies can hedge their positions using currency futures. For instance, a US company expecting payment in euros for goods sold to a French client can use currency futures to hedge against potential losses due to exchange rate fluctuations, ensuring they receive the expected amount in US dollars.

Speculative traders can also use Currency futures as they look to profit from anticipated changes in exchange rates. For example, if a trader expects the euro to strengthen against the US dollar in the foreseeable, they can buy euro currency futures contracts to capitalise on the potential appreciation. The ability to leverage positions through margin makes currency futures attractive to speculators seeking enhanced exposure to those exchange rate movements.

Let's take a look at that in an example.

CURRENCY FUTURES - WORKED EXAMPLE

Consider the example involving the Euro / Dollar futures contract, which, for reference, has the ticker name 6E, from a speculator's viewpoint. Suppose you purchase 8 Euro contracts, each representing €125,000, at a rate of 0.96 US$/€. By the end of the day, the settlement price rose to 0.98 US$/€. To calculate your profit, you would use the following formula:

(Settlement Price-Initial Price) × Contract Size × Number of Contracts

Woah, slow down, X.

I've got you. Math incoming.

(0.98 US$/€ - 0.96 US$/€) x €125,000 x 8 = $20,000

See, nothing to worry about.

In this scenario, the increase in the price results in a profit of $20,000. Now, of course, that would be a big move, so what you need to be aware of with any contract is the tick incremental change and tick value. These specifications all form part of the standardisation to each contract. What this means is each tick move in any contract will represent a specific dollar value. In the case of the Euro Dollar FX contract, it's as follows.

Tick Change: 0.000050
Tick Value: $6.25

In Leyman's, if 1 contract were to move 100 ticks, you would effectively gain $625.

Time to break down the example above. The difference between the purchase price of 0.96 and the sale price of 0.98 is 0.02. So, dividing 0.02 by the tick size (0.000050) leaves you with 400 ticks.

Then, go back to the tick value of $6.25 per tick.

400 ticks x $6.25 tick value = $2,500

How many contracts? 8. So:

8 x 2,500 = $20,000

Now, go and create your own hypothetical trade in the notes!

TICKER LIST

Here are some of the most popular Currency Futures.

6J1! - Continuous Contract Japanese Yen Futures

6B1! - Continuous Contract British Pound Futures

6C1! - Continuous Contract Canadian Dollar Futures

6M1! - Continuous Contract Mexican Pesos Futures

BTC1! - Continuous Contract Bitcoin Futures

ETH1! - Continuous Contract Ethereum Futures

6S1 - Continuous Contract Swiss Franc Futures

6E1! - Continuous Euro FX Futures

For a complete list, review **https://www.tradingview.com/markets/futures/quotes-currencies/**

3-step representation of every Trader throughout their career;

Severe Struggle,
Moderate Struggle,
Struggle

Solution?

Find consistency in the struggle.

ENERGY

Among the wide selection of energy futures contracts listed on the NYMEX exchange, covering categories like coal, electricity, ethanol, crude oil, natural gas, and refined products, there are five standout leaders in terms of daily trading volume. These top contenders are West Texas Crude Oil, Brent Crude Oil, Reformulated Unleaded Gas, Henry Hub Natural Gas, and Ultra-Low Sulphur Diesel, commonly known as Heating Oil.

Like all futures contracts, energy futures are also leveraged products that aid in providing greater trading opportunities for investors who are seeking to capitalise from leverage. In short, when you utilise a futures contract, you benefit from the ability to manage and control large positions by leveraging relatively small amounts of capital deployed. For example, picking up on Crude Oil, a single Crude Oil futures contract controls 1,000 barrels of the commodity; which, if the underlying was trading at $90 per barrel, would give you, as the trader, control of a notional contract value worth $90,000.

Taking Ninja Trader's margin requirements as an example, you can control that $90,000 with an initial margin of $7260. Pretty crazy, right? Now, if you throw in the influence of energy products in our daily lives along with the geopolitical tensions across the world, which often directly affect the Energy Markets, think wars, and you can see why it's no surprise that Energy Futures rank among the most heavily traded futures contracts globally. It's a fun anecdote, but given the sheer volatility provided by global political jostling and constant threats of regional unrest, in Crude Oil specifically, there are literally tankers out at sea, completely non-operational, i.e., not moving, yet simply storing vast quantities of barrels in Crude Oil for future release. If you can't see it, it doesn't exist, right? Right.

Now if you engage in these markets, you can imagine who, what and where is storing your Oil.

I've placed a link in the Sources section found at the back of this book, which will take you to an image of the Karvounis, a Suezman-sized tanker, which, according to Reuters in 2020, was held outside Port Fourchon in Louisiana, U.S.

As a side note, in 2020, record barrels were held offshore. 160 million barrels to be exact. Now that's a lot of Barrels.

WHAT ARE ENERGY FUTURES USED FOR?

As you will have assumed by now, the energy futures contract has become an essential part of the modern financial system over the decades thanks to its efficiency in controlling volatility in the price of underlying commodities such as coal and gas. This is done by futures contracts setting pricing benchmarks globally. For example, WTI Crude, Henry Hub Natural Gas, and Brent Crude futures are widely used to establish pricing curves and manage risk in the energy markets. It'll be interesting to see how this develops in the future as the world moves away from fossil fuels, but that being said, for now anyway, futures contracts still offer an effective hedging and diversification tool used for risk management that is ideal for investors, consumers, and providers to hedge or speculate. They are also used as geopolitical bargaining chips, but let's not go there, ey.

In commercial terms, an energy futures contract is a derivative contract established between two parties to buy or sell energy products or commodities at a predetermined date and price for future delivery. As a reminder, derivatives are financial instruments whose values are derived from underlying assets. In the case of energy futures, these underlying assets comprise energy products such as crude oil, natural gas, and electricity. For investors like you and I, energy futures offer the opportunity to speculate on price movements caused by macroeconomic and geopolitical conditions.

HOW DO ENERGY FUTURES WORK?

Let's now consider an example in a commercial hedging sense. In steps, the hypothetical natural gas producer, "MuchoGasCo," seeking to hedge 10,000 million British thermal units (MMBtu) of its February production.

MuchGasCo could achieve this by selling one New York Mercantile Exchange (NYMEX) natural gas futures contract (ticker NG.) Suppose MuchoGasCo sells the contract at a price of $3.822 per MMBtu at market closing. This action effectively hedges 10,000 MMBtu of MuchoGasCo's February production at $3.822 per MMBtu. To avoid physical delivery, MuchoGasCo would repurchase one February futures contract on or before the expiration date of the initial agreement.

If the market price at buyback is $4 per MMBtu, MuchoGasCo would incur a hedging loss of $0.172 per MMBtu as the price has increased but would receive $4 per MMBtu for its physical natural gas.

On the other hand, if the market price at buyback was $3 per MMBtu, MuchoGasCo would realise a hedging gain of $0.822 per MMBtu as price declined in line with the selling of the futures contract, whilst also receiving $3 per MMBtu for its physical natural gas.

You can see here that in both scenarios, the gross profit remains $3.822 per MMBtu. Now, of course, this is unlikely in real terms, but the premise should help you understand the hedging nature companies can deploy to mitigate risks within their businesses. This hedging approach is, of course, applicable to both oil and gas producers and consumers.

For example, energy end-users seeking to hedge their exposure to potentially higher energy prices would employ an opposite approach. Instead of selling energy futures like producers do, the consumer or end-user would buy energy futures contracts to lock in prices. Generally, while some details will need ironing out before buying or selling futures contracts in a commercial sense, the mechanism is straightforward: buy energy futures contracts to hedge against potential price increases and sell them when energy prices are declining as a hedge.

As a speculator, you don't need to worry about the hedging aspect of futures markets. All a speculator is looking to do is predict the direction of the underlying asset and seek to gain from such movements.

Different types of energy futures contracts are available for investors. Earlier, we touched on Standardisation, here, we'll look at it in more detail. Each contract type is standardised, i.e., it has its underlying commodity, contract size, tick size, and expiration date. There are also Micro versions with their own specification to consider, which are essentially a fraction of the standard contracts size. Below, I've outlined some specifications for Energy Futures Contracts to give you an appreciation of Standardisation. I'll show an example of how to use this in a practical sense straight after.

Some popular Energy Futures contracts:

Crude Oil Futures: The underlying commodity for this futures contract is WTI (West Texas Intermediate) crude oil. Each contract represents 1,000 US barrels, equivalent to 42,000 gallons of oil. The tick size, which denotes the minimum price movement, is 1 cent per barrel, translating to $10 per contract. This futures contract expires on the third business day before the 25th calendar day of the month preceding the delivery month. It is predominantly traded on NYMEX (the New York Mercantile Exchange) under the ticker symbol CL. There is also the popular MCL contract, which is the Micro version of the standard contract representing 1/10th the size. It controls 100 barrels with a 0.01 tick size, equating to $1 per contract.

Brent Crude Oil Futures: So, the underlying commodity for this futures contract is Brent crude oil. Each contract represents 1,000 US barrels, equivalent to 42,000 gallons of oil. The tick size, indicating the minimum price movement, is also 1 cent per barrel, equal to $10 per contract. This futures contract, like Crude Oil, expires on the last business day of the second month preceding the delivery month. It is primarily traded on the Intercontinental Exchange (ICE) under the ticker symbol BRN.

Henry Hub Natural Gas Futures: It is arguably the least popular out of the three mentioned here by speculators, but the underlying commodity for this futures contract is natural gas, with its pricing based on the Louisiana Henry Hub natural gas price. This futures contract, symbolised as NG, is the most prominent global natural gas future and is traded on the New York Mercantile Exchange (NYMEX). Each contract has a size of 10,000 MMBtu (Million British Thermal Units). The tick size, which denotes the minimum price movement, is 0.0001 per MMBtu, equivalent to $10 per contract. The contract expires three business days before the first calendar day of the delivery month.

Okay, so here's a worked exampled for Crude Oil bringing it all together.

ENERGY FUTURES - WORKED EXAMPLE

As a wrap-up, understanding your tick size, contract size, and the current price of your contract can help you calculate your profit or loss. As an example, the WTI crude oil contract has a tick size of $0.01 per barrel and a standardisation of 1,000 US barrels, as outlined above.

So, if the current price of WTI futures is $74.50 per barrel, the contract value for 1 contract is given by calculating the following:

Current price x Contract size

Or:

$74.5 per barrel x 1,000 barrels = $74,500

Contract Value

The dollar value of a one-tick move, known as the Incremental Tick Value, is calculated using the following:

Tick size x Contract size

Or:

$0.01 x 1,000 = $10 per tick

Therefore, if you initially bought one WTI contract at $73 and the current price is $74.50.

You would calculate your profit per contract as follows:

$74.50 (Current Price) - $73 (Purchase Price) = $1.5

In short, your contract has moved $1.50.

To work out how many ticks it has moved. Divide that number by tick size:

$1.50 / $0.01 = 150 ticks

To calculate your profit / loss, multiply your tick gain / loss by the value per tick:

150 ticks x $10 per tick = $1,500

Should you hold multiple contracts, calculate your total profit by multiplying the per-contract gain by the number of contracts:

Number of contracts x $1,500

So, if you bought 1 contract, you would have made $1,500, 2 Contracts $3000, and so on.

Now, if you traded MCL, which is the Micro contract, simply divide the number by 10.

TICKER LIST

Here are some of the most popular Energy Futures.

CL1! - Continuous Contract Crude Oil Futures

BR1! - Continuous Contract Brent Crude Futures

NG1! - Continuous Contract Henry Hub Natural Gas Futures

For a complete list, review **https://www.tradingview.com/markets/futures/quotes-energy/**

FUTURES ASSET CLASSES - ENERGY

*Being poor is tough,
being rich is tough...
Make a choice.*

FINANCIALS

While the likelihood of engaging directly in trading financial futures may be low, it's still valuable to understand them or at least know what they are. Personally, I don't actively trade financial futures being content in the asset classes I do trade; however, I do monitor closely. Bonds, in particular, exhibit an inverse correlation with the DXY (US Dollar Index). This relationship holds significance in analysing other asset classes I focus on, such as indexes and metals. This interconnectedness provides insights into broader market movements and helps inform trading strategies across various asset classes.

That being said, financial futures are, again, derivatives contracts associated with underlying assets that, in this case, are interest-bearing instruments. On U.S. exchanges, these futures contracts encompass a range of maturities, with examples including the 30-year Treasury Bond and the 10-year Treasury Note, both traded on the Chicago Board of Trade (CBOT). Now, as a general overview, interest rate futures are financial derivatives that are designed to provide investors with exposure to fluctuations in interest rates. When interest rates rise, the value of an interest rate futures contract typically declines. This occurs as higher interest rates increase the appeal of new debt instruments being offered by the government, causing existing bonds to lose value as their interest rates become less competitive.

Consequently, the prices of existing bonds decrease to align with the higher rates. On the other hand, declining interest rates can bolster the value of an interest rate futures contract. In such instances, lower interest rates make existing bonds more attractive, leading to an increase in the prices of these bonds and, as a net result, in the value of interest rate futures contracts.

HOW DO FINANCIAL FUTURES WORK?

Interest rate futures have various underlying instruments, including Treasury bills (T-bills), which represent short-term lending backed by the US government, and Treasury bonds (T-bonds), which represent long-term lending backed by the US government. As promised at the start of the book, I want to avoid overly techy topics, but if you want to learn more about T-Bonds and T-Bills, I've laid out some more info in the glossary, which can be found at the back of the book.

T-bill futures are traded on the Chicago Mercantile Exchange (CME). In contrast, T-bond futures are available on the Chicago Board of Trade (CBOT), another division of the CME. Additionally, certificates of deposit (CDs) and Treasury note securities serve as underlying assets for interest rate futures. Among the most popular interest rate futures are those based on various long-term Treasury maturities, including the 30-year, 10-year, 5-year, and 2-year Treasuries. These futures contracts provide the investors with opportunities to hedge against interest rate fluctuations and speculate on changes in interest rates across different durations and markets.

Participants in the financial futures market encompass a diverse background - similar to all other futures markets, ranging, of course, from large institutional hedgers seeking to manage risk associated with interest rate exposures to speculators aiming to capitalise on accurately predicting the direction of rate movements. In doing so, interest rate futures contracts enable buyers and sellers to secure rates on interest-bearing assets, such as government bonds. Although physical delivery of these types of assets doesn't occur, their worth is linked to the underlying asset's price. When interest rates rise, the value of existing bonds decreases as their fixed rates become less appealing.

One popular type of interest rate futures is Treasury bond futures, where the underlying asset is a US Treasury bond with a face value of $100,000 and a remaining term of at least 15 years until maturity. We'll look at this in an example shortly, but for clarity, the purpose of these futures contracts is to provide participants with a means to hedge against interest rate fluctuations and speculate on changes in bond prices tied to shifts in interest rates.

WHAT ARE FINANCIAL FUTURES USED FOR?

The best way to explain this is via an example. Consider a scenario where a fund manager holds a large quantity of long-term US Treasury bonds and anticipates that T-bond prices may decline in the event of rising interest rates in the coming months. To hedge against this risk, the manager can opt to sell Treasury bond futures contracts, effectively locking in prices to sell at a future date.

So, should interest rates indeed increase as anticipated, the prices of the manager's Treasury portfolio would likely decrease. However, the gains from their short futures position would counterbalance this loss. By taking this approach, that same investor can mitigate their exposure to fluctuations in interest rates without the necessity of liquidating their bond holdings.

Speculators might adopt a different stance, however, by purchasing futures contracts with the expectation that interest rates will decrease. In this scenario, if interest rates do indeed decline, treasury bond prices would rise, resulting in increased prices for their long futures contracts. Upon expiration, these contracts settle in cash based on the prevailing market price, with no physical bonds changing hands. But as always, exiting before settlement is an option, too.

Personally, I use this asset class as a metric for analysing the overall health of the market, supporting my analysis in relation to directional bias when trading Index Futures. To give you an idea, when Bonds decrease, weakness often enters the US stock market as interest rates are predicted to rise. This, in turn, affects the direction of the S&P 500 futures derivative contract, ES. Anticipation of higher interest rates in the future causes companies to reconsider growth strategies as borrowing becomes more expensive. Higher interest rates is often a sign of an unhealthy economy, too, with a net result being consumers having less disposable income to spend on those companies concerned about increased borrowing costs. You see how it's all connected!

> *Here's a little guide for you to use in your own trading. As a dis-claimer. I'm not a financial advisor so do ensure you carry out your own due diligence before committing money into the markets. However, generally, when bonds go down, interest rate yields go up along with the US dollar. Index Futures have an inverse correlation to the Dollar. I.e., they'll move down. Now, when bonds increase, yields are likely to decrease along with the US dollar. Again, Index Futures have an inverse correlation. I.e., likely to go up.*
>
> *For clarity, I'll use this in-formation to support my overall bias when considering long-term trends. I've inserted an image of my chart that tracks these instruments below as to provide a visual representation.*

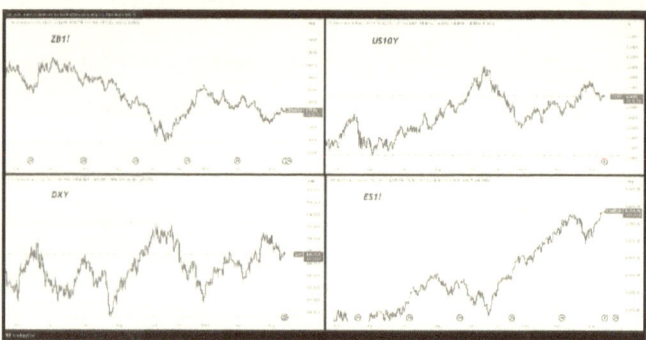

Credit; Trading View Charts, Profile: The_real_Trade_X

FINANCIAL FUTURES - WORKED EXAMPLE

The face value of most Treasury's is $100,000. So, the contract size for a Treasury-based interest rate future is usually $100,000. Each contract trades in handles of $1,000, split into increments ($1,000 ÷ 32).

If a quote on a contract is listed as 101'25 (or often listed as 101-25), this would mean the total price of the contract is the face value plus one handle plus 25/32 of another handle:

101'25 Price = $100,000 + $1,000 + ($1,000 × 25|32) = $101,781.25

Now, it's worth noting that the Eurodollar works slightly differently - in $25 increments. So, replace 32 with 25, and the handle size is $2500 vs $1000.

TICKER LIST

Here are some of the most popular Interest Rate Futures.

ZB1! - Continuous Contract US Treasury Bond

ZN1! - Continuous Contract 10Y T-Note Futures

For a complete list, review **https://www.tradingview.com/markets/futures/quotes-interest-rates/**

Becoming who you most want to be is SIMPLE.
BUT, becoming who you most want to be is not EASY.

METALS

Now, you'll probably be getting nauseous with me saying this, but here goes. Metal futures are contracts that allow traders to buy or sell a specific amount of a metal at a predetermined price and date in the future and are traded on commodity exchanges, such as the London Metal Exchange (LME) and the New York Mercantile Exchange (NYMEX), and as you guessed it, are used by producers and consumers of metals, such as mining companies and manufacturers, to hedge against price fluctuations and manage risk. Traders can also use metal futures to speculate on price movements and profit from market fluctuations, with contracts spanning various metals such as copper, gold, silver, platinum, and palladium. Are you grasping the concept of futures yet?

As is the case with those mentioned previously; in order to trade metal futures, a trader must open a futures trading account with a broker and deposit funds to cover the margin requirements. Margin, for clarity, is the amount of money required to hold a futures position and is typically a small percentage of the total contract value.

In the case of Gold's full-size contract, (Ticker: GC), this would be $11,000 as an initial margin. However, that $11,000 will enable you to control essentially 1 brick of physical gold, or in other words, 100 Troy ounces. So, the true dollar value in this contract would be 100 times the market price of gold; whatever 1 ounce of gold is trading at that given time. Today, that would give you a contract value worth $231,000 worth of gold. We'll look at the benefits and pitfalls of using margin shortly.

Now, I'm going to focus on gold in this section as it's the commodity I most often trade, but the principles are replicable across all the metals.

WHAT ARE METAL FUTURES USED FOR?

The primary purpose is to establish a centralised platform for individuals or entities interested in purchasing or selling precious metals at a future date. Metal futures play a crucial role in helping hedgers mitigate risks associated with adverse price fluctuations in the cash (physical) market. Examples of hedgers include bank vaults, mines, manufacturers, and jewelers. An interesting fact is that COMEX, one of the largest exchanges, facilitates delivery and, therefore, stores vast quantities of physical gold within the vaults in New York. No wonder we have so many *Mission Impossible* movies, huh!

For clarity though, hedgers typically take positions in the futures market that are opposite to their physical holdings, thanks to the price correlation between futures and spot markets. Gains in one market can offset losses in the other. For instance, a jeweller concerned about potential price hikes in gold might purchase a futures contract to lock in a guaranteed price. If the market price rises, they'll have to pay more for gold or silver; however, since they took a long position in futures, they could profit from the contract, offsetting the increased cost.

If gold prices decrease, the hedger might incur losses on futures contracts but pay less in the cash market for gold or silver.

Contrasting to hedgers, and realistically where most traders reside, in speculation, aim to profit without intending to take physical delivery. Speculators, by the way can include individual investors, hedge funds, or commodity trading advisors (CTAs).

Gold futures contracts are traded on various exchanges worldwide, with notable ones including the COMEX division of the New York Mercantile Exchange (NYMEX), which, as you'll now be aware, is a subdivision of CME, the Tokyo Commodity Exchange (TOCOM), and the Shanghai Futures Exchange (SHFE). Consequently, different exchanges use slightly different tickers for gold futures. While personal preferences may vary, and for me, that's with CME, it's essential to recognise that all these exchanges provide centralised platforms for buyers and sellers to engage in trading gold futures.

HOW METALS FUTURES WORK?

Suppose you like to hold your Bullion. In that case, although it's possible with Gold futures by notifying the exchange you'd like to take delivery on the settlement date, as speculators, chances are you won't see any. Why, I hear you ask. Well, Gold futures differ from physical ownership given that the contracts are notable for their standardisation, and so the quantities of physical gold can be vast. Typically denominated in troy ounces, each contract outlines the precise quantity of gold for delivery alongside specifying the minimum purity level. For instance, a single gold futures contract typically represents 100 troy ounces of 24-karat gold. It's done this way via standardisation to provide structure to the market by streamlining the contract comparison and trading process. This, in turn, provides accessibility and liquidity to the market. An approach used across asset classes I might add.

Gold futures also have defined expiration dates, determining when the contract will be settled. The most actively traded contracts typically have expiration dates in the near future, 3 months usually. In contrast, contracts with longer expiry dates tend to have noticeably lower trading volumes. My advice is to stick to the current contract, regardless of what asset you are trading. I'll go into how to search for the current contract by using ticker codes later.

For now, let's bring in the concept of leverage, or margin, as already mentioned earlier, so you can understand how that plays its role and look at the difference between holding your bullion (physical ownership) and Futures Trading (Gold Futures). In short, margin allows for leverage (also known as gearing) on the underlying asset.

WORKED EXAMPLE - GOLD FUTURES

Consider this scenario: Suppose you have $10,000 available for investment. With that amount, you could obviously purchase gold bullion worth $10,000. However, with gold futures, you might be able to leverage up to $200,000! This is possible because the margin requirement for a $200,000 futures contract is typically around 5%, equating to $10,000.

Now, imagine the underlying price increases by 10%. If you invested in physical bullion, you'd gain $1000, whereas with gold futures, your profit would be $20,000.

Sounds enticing, right? But always remember, there's a flip side. If the price of gold drops by 10%, your loss would be limited to $1000 with bullion, and your investment would remain intact, potentially recouping losses if gold rebounds in the future.

However, with futures, that same 10% decrease translates to a $20,000 loss—$10,000 more than your initial investment. You might be prompted to inject additional funds as a margin top-up, and if the loss hits $30,000, you might be compelled to close your position, losing your entire investment.

However, if you choose not to top-up your margin, your broker could close your position, and you'd lose your original $10,000. Ouch!

This highlights why futures can be perilous for those overly confident in their predictions, especially those trading with personal funds. The harsh reality is the majority of futures traders end up losing money. Futures pose a significant threat to wealth if not managed properly and are therefore, one of the reasons why holding Physical Gold is seen as such a "safe haven.'

Now, to work out how the price of a gold futures contract moves, you need to consider the specifications of the contract once again. It's standardisation. You can always find this information with your chosen broker by reviewing the specific asset and toggling through to the specifications list. Alternatively, you can go onto the CME website and search for the assets' specifications. But to run through gold briefly;

Tick Size: 0.10 cents

Tick Value: $10

So, for every $1 move in the underlying equates to $100.

For example, if you bought GC at 5,000 and sold it for 5010, you would profit $1000:

$100 x 10 = $1000

So, let's conclude here by noting that gold futures are different from physical gold ownership. When trading these contracts, the focus is on price movement and profit potential rather than physical possession. It is, of course, possible to take delivery of physical gold by holding the contract until its expiry and notifying the exchange of your intention to take delivery. But in most cases, you will settle prior to the settlement date. Maybe add that one to your bucket list! Getting the vaults in New York to send you 100 Troy Ounces of 24kt Gold after taking a contract through to settlement. Now that deserves an, a bosh!

TICKER LIST

Here are some of the most popular Metal Futures.

GC1! - Continuous Contract Gold Futures

AG1! - Continuous Contract Silver Futures

AL1! - Continuous Contract Aluminum Futures

For a complete list, review **https://www.tradingview.com/markets/futures/quotes-metals/**

Inaction breeds doubt and fear...
Action breeds confidence and courage

GRAINS

Among all available futures contracts traded on US exchanges, those tied to tangible commodities, grain futures are the quintessential asset class. Why? Because these contracts have historical significance as they were instrumental in establishing the initial central marketplaces where farmers and buyers could transact corn under standardised procedures for grading and weighing their crops. This initial process facilitated industry expansion as producers and purchasers sought stability in their investments. Interesting, right?

As these commitments for future transactions became the norm among farmers and buyers, the evolution of futures contracts began. Agreed-upon contracts could now be bought and sold before the specified date, providing flexibility for those concerned throughout the crop year. Today, markets for wheat, corn, oats, soybeans, and their primary by-products—soybean oil and soybean meal—are substantial.

Given the significant impact of weather conditions on crop quality, grain futures markets are known for their volatility. These complexities make grain futures among the most dynamic and volatile markets traded today.

HOW DO GRAIN FUTURES WORK?

Let's again look at them from a basic level and why they exist.

At their core, they are agricultural commodities such as corn, soybeans, and wheat, as mentioned above. I've placed a complete list below. Grain futures are legally binding contracts for the delivery of a particular grain for a specified price at some point in the future. Like the contracts mentioned previously, contracts are standardised and traded on centralised exchanges. One such exchange is CBOT (short from the Chicago Board of Exchanges).

Now, a key driver for the grain market is to allow farmers to lock in prices before harvest. Still, there are generally two reasons for dealing with grain futures.

So, who might consider trading grains? Well, first, a speculator - such as me, may wish to make a profit by predicting grain price movements, much as a stock trader makes a profit by correctly predicting that his equity will increase in value or by anticipating an increase in Gold futures due to instability in the US currency. If a trader takes a long position on wheat – and a supply disruption causes the price of wheat bushels to rise significantly – that trader can benefit from the shift increase in price.

Secondly, on a commercial level, producers and consumers may wish to trade grain futures as a hedge against an existing position to mitigate risk associated with future availability or price swings.

Remember, grains fall into the physical futures category, so speculators who do not intend to take delivery, or indeed supply corn, wheat, or soy should exit their positions before the settlement date when trading with personal capital.

For clarity, one of the benefits of trading futures contracts is that they allow for more leverage than trading the actual commodity. One futures contract for soybeans represents 5,000 bushels. Like gold discussed above, traders can control larger positions with less capital. One thing to note about the grain market is that it offers good opportunities for those with limited capital, as grain futures also have lower margins than other commodity counterparts. This is due to contracts being lower in total dollar amount.

Here's the list of commonly traded Grains:

Corn / Soybeans / Wheat / Oats / Soybean oil / Soymeal / Rice

GRAIN FUTURES - WORKED EXAMPLES

For example, if a soybean futures contract allows the trader to control 5,000 bushels, and bushels are trading at $7 each, the dollar value of the contract is $35,000.

Another example would be to look at corn. The CME corn contract represents 5,000 bushels. So, for instance, if corn is trading at $2.50 per bushel, the contract's value would be $12,500:

5,000 bushels x $2.50 = $12,500

If a trader buys at $2.50 and sells at $2.60, they'd profit $500:

$2.60 - $2.50 = 10 cents

10 cents x 5,000 = $500

Now, of course, if they sell at $2.40 after buying at $2.50, they'd incur a $500 loss.

In essence, each penny difference equals a $50 upward or downward movement.

Corn is priced in dollars and cents, with the minimum tick size set at $0.0025 (one-quarter of a cent), equating to $12.50 per contract. This tick size is combined with volatility; when corn moves in $ movements, the potential for significant financial gain and loss can be realised.

The most active delivery months for corn include March, May, July, September, and December.

TICKER LIST

Here are some of the most popular Grain Futures.

ZW1! - Continuous Contract Wheat Futures

ZS1! - Continuous Contract Soybean Futures

ZC - Corn Futures

For a complete list, review **https://www.tradingview.com/markets/futures/quotes-agricultural/**

MEATS

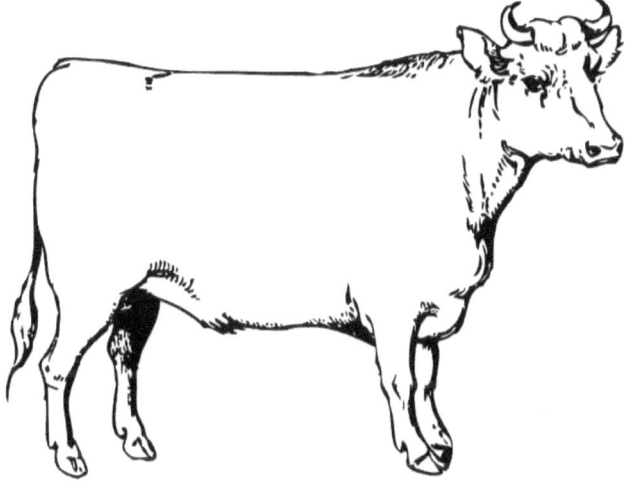

Something I learnt recently regarding livestock futures was the prominence of the once-iconic commodity, Pork Bellies. Although they still reside on many a table around the world, sorry, vegans! This futures contract is now just a distant memory when it was delisted in 2011. See, Vegans, immediate Karma! However, Pork Bellies actually once dominated the trading pit at the Chicago Mercantile Exchange during its peak in the late '70s and early '80s.

Nowadays, Lean Hogs has taken its place as the go-to futures contract for most of the pork traders. Meanwhile, for those interested in beef, Live Cattle and Feeder Cattle contracts are also among the available options. It's good to note that grains, meats, and soft commodities (discussed later) all fall under the umbrella of Agriculture Futures. Those Chinese Dolls at it again.

WHAT ARE MEAT FUTURES USED FOR?

Meat Futures, commonly known as Livestock futures, offer farmers, meat packers, processors, and traders a means to hedge against the risks of price volatility in the livestock market. By locking in the price for future delivery, these market participants can mitigate their risks and plan their operations more accurately.

HOW DO MEAT FUTURES WORK?

An example described in Steven, C Blank Article on *LiveStock Futures using Futures or Options;*

For a Livestock producer, hedging involves locking in the value of animals to be sold in the cash market sometime in the future by selling futures contracts. The hedging process would be as follows;

For example, for live cattle, each contract covers a standardised quantity of 40,000 pounds and specifies quality. If producers establish a hedge, the net effect would be to minimise any potential loss against the net fluctuation in cattle prices at the settlement date.

MEAT FUTURES - WORKED EXAMPLE

Steven goes on to say; Hypothetically, a producer is anticipating he will have 40000 pounds of cattle in April. He could expect a cash price of 75 cents/lb and seek to lock in the cash price by selling a futures contract. If cash values drop between the contract settlement date and the date the contract was sold, that future contract increase would offset the 10c/lb drop in the underlying asset. The net result would be a 10c gain.

This would also be true if the underlying (cash price) increased by 10 c, given the producer had already locked in prices with the futures contract. In this example, this would result in a net revenue of $29,950.

Now there is a far more advanced way of looking at Meat Futures from a commercial viewpoint which includes basis points. This is a set sum the consumer, such as meat packers or producers, would have to pay in his location above the current futures contract price. But as promised from the start, I want to avoid overly complex topics that aren't essential for day-to-day trading. If you really want to dive into this topic as you're considering opening a meat processing plant, I have placed a link in the sources section.

TICKER LIST

Here are some of the most popular Meat Futures.

LE - Live Cattle Futures
BG1! - Feeder cattle Futures
ZC - Corn Futures

For a complete list, review **https://www.tradingview.com/markets/futures/quotes-agricultural/**

SOFTS

Cocoa, coffee, cotton, orange juice, and sugar—futures contracts, along with grains, are among some of the oldest commodities traded in the market. They represent essential products that we all consume daily and, as a result, provide valuable opportunities in the game of futures trading.

The prevailing direction of these commodities is deeply intertwined with weather conditions, much like the prevailing wind, which can have both beneficial and adverse effects on crop yields. Either way, it's worth noting that these weather-related factors lead to significant price fluctuations. We only need to look at cocoa today to see how the effects of weather conditions resulting in a lack of supply and increasing demand can cause incredible movements. In the case of cocoa, nearly 1000% in a year. Yikes!

WHAT ARE SOFT FUTURES USED FOR?

Farmers rely on these futures contracts to secure stable prices for their crops amidst the unpredictability of weather patterns, diseases, and other agricultural risks, just like in the case of grains. Meanwhile, speculative investors are looking to navigate the fluctuating prices of soft commodities.

Let's be clear: the volatility of soft commodity futures is undeniable, set in motion mainly by factors including weather forecasts, planting and harvesting reports, and the ever-changing demands of global markets. These fluctuations can profoundly affect the value of contracts, driving prices up or down depending on the timing and severity of these external influences. But here lays a distinct difference: this difference from geological deposits found in hard commodities, if you recall, is what separates the two subcategories, both of which are intrinsic to the respective asset class. For completeness, it should be mentioned that softs, grains, and meats often fall under the category of agricultural commodities, so the distinction between softs can differ between exchanges, although the principles of the categories remain. Lumber is one example which often gets shoehorned into classes unbeknownst. If you use TradingView as your platform for charting, you will find Orange Juice alongside Live Cattle in the Agriculture category, for example. But returning to softs and weather implications, a sudden shift in weather patterns or a report indicating decreased crop levels can swiftly alter the trajectory of prices, which is why farmers, producers, manufacturers, and consumers utilise the Futures market to either manage risk, hedge, or speculate on said fluctuations.

Let's look at some worked examples, starting with the soft future contract which has had the most incredible move across the futures markets in the past year. As I'm writing, it's 2024. Simply go and look at cocoa (Ticker: CC) if you want to see first-hand the volatility in futures markets.

COCOA

Cocoa is traded in dollars per metric ton and one contract is for 10 metric tons, so when cocoa is trading at $2,000/M ton, the contract has a total value of $20,000. If a trader is long at $2,000/M ton, and the markets move to $2,100/M ton, you'd calculate profit as follows:

$$($2,100 - $2,000 = $100)$$

$$100 \times 10 \text{ M ton.} = $1,000 \text{ profit}$$

The minimum tick size is a dollar, equating to $10 per contract. Often, the market will trade in increments greater than a dollar, but one dollar is the smallest amount it can move.

To put this into perspective. As of writing, cocoa has moved from c$2,000 in September 2022 to nearly $10,000 in March 2024.

Not to make you weep, but if you had bought 1 contract in late 2023, you would have made $80,000 as of today.

($10,000 - $2,000 = $8000)

8000 x 10 Mton = $80,000 profit

Now that certainly deserves an A BOSH!

COFFEE

We all love coffee, but how will it work in the futures markets? Let's cover it. Coffee is traded in cents per pound, and one contract of coffee controls 37,500 pounds of coffee.

When the price of coffee is trading at $1/pound, the cash value of that contract will be:

$37,500 ($1.00 x 37,500 = $37,500)

The tick size is 5 cents per pound, which equates to $18.75 per tick.

For example, if a trader went long at $1.1000 and the markets moved to $1.1550, the trader would have a profit of:

$2062.50 ($1.1550 - $1.1000 = $0.0550, and $0.0550 x 37,500 = $2,062.50)

COTTON

Cotton is traded in 50,000-pound contracts. It is also traded in cents per pound, so if the market is trading at 53 cents per pound, the contract will have a value of $26,500:

$0.53 x 50,000 pounds = $26,500

The minimum tick size is $0.0001 or $5 per contract.

Therefore, any 2-cent move in cotton will equate to either a gain or a loss of $1,000. When cotton prices exceed 95 cents per pound, the minimum tick movement will expand to $0.0005 to accommodate larger daily ranges.

TICKER LIST

Here are some of the most popular Soft Futures.

CE1! - Cocoa Futures

OJ1! - Orange Juice Futures

ZC1! - Corn Futures

For a complete list, review **https://www.tradingview.com/markets/futures/quotes-agricultural/**

*There is a time to go long,
A time to go short,
And a time to go fishing...*

— JESSE LIVERMORE

INDICES

So, if you ever thought about trading with (or against me) ouch, then it's here, with Index futures where you will find me - the majority of the time trading every day, and let's be clear, it's not just me. As mentioned at the start, these are some of the more heavily traded futures contracts among speculative traders, and to be honest, it's not surprising. Among all the financial instruments we can think of in the world, stock indexes are the most often discussed globally. The list is extensive, and we have access to global markets. For example, the Nikkei 225, commonly known as the Nikkei is the stock market index for Tokyo. We also have the DAX for Germany or the Nifty 50 for India. In short, regardless of where you want to deploy your capital, you have an option.

WHAT IS AN INDEX?

An index is simply a measurement of the price of a single item or a collection of assets - such is the case with the Indices. For example, the S&P 500 (Standard & Poor 500) tracks the stock performance of the largest 500 companies listed on the Stock Exchange in the United States. It serves as a crucial benchmark for assessing overall health in the US stock market and the broader economy. Investors and economists often rely on the S&P

500 as a key economic indicator (Metric) as it reflects collective investor expectations for the future, contrasting with other economic data that depict present or recent economic conditions. References to the US "stock market" commonly denote the S&P 500, accurately representing the performance of large-cap or blue-chip stocks.

In the US markets, we also have the Nasdaq 100 and Dow Jones, so let's take a look at them.

NASDAQ 100

As a snapshot - the Nasdaq 100, with Futures Contract (Ticker: NQ), is traded on the Chicago Mercantile Exchange and is a stock market index comprising the shares of the 100 largest US and international companies, excluding those from the financial sector. The Nasdaq 100 is measured by market capitalisation and is well known for representing the largest tech stocks. E-mini and Micro Nasdaq futures are available for trading almost around the clock at the same times as the S&P 500. We'll look at the contract differences shortly. For now, it's worth knowing that of all the Index Futures available, I'd argue the Nasdaq 100 is the most volatile.

DOW JONES INDUSTRIAL AVERAGE

The Dow Jones Industrial Average (DJIA) with Futures Contract (Ticker: YM) is a stock market index that monitors the performance of 30 major publicly owned blue chip companies traded on both the New York Stock Exchange (NYSE) and Nasdaq. Originating in 1896, Charles Dow established the index in collaboration with his business partner Edward Jones, hence its name. It's not one I trade particularly often, as I tend to stick with the S&P 500 and Nasdaq 100. However, it's still one I track for confluences depicting overall strength or weakness in the US Market.

Now let's be clear: we're not limited to the US market only as previously mentioned; there are Indexes galore—for example, the Nifty 50 tracks the top 50 largest companies in India. The FTSE 100 Index tracks the top 100 most capitalised blue chip companies on the London Stock Exchange and so on. Your choices are almost endless. However, for me, I tend to focus on the US Markets given so much of the world is controlled by the US dollar.

WHAT ARE INDEX FUTURES?

Index Futures on the other hand, are derivatives. All this means is they are based on the underlying asset, (Index). So, in the purest sense, a trader can speculate on the specific asset's (Index's) future appreciation or depreciation by using the futures derivative. In the case of the S&P 500, an investor could buy or sell the Index future, ticker name (ES), or in the case of Nasdaq 100, ticker name (NQ).

To find the current month, or any month for that matter, of an asset you are looking to trade, understand the following (Ticker:Month:Year). Therefore, if you were looking to trade the E-Mini S&P500 - which is the S&P 500 Futures contract, on the June Contract, you'd be trading ESM2024.

Here is a breakdown of the month codes for your reference:
March: Code H
June: Code M
September: Code U
December: Code Z
Remember the formula (Ticker:Month:Year)

Unlike other futures contracts, stock index futures contracts do not involve physical delivery, as we touched on previously. Instead, the contracts are cash-settled, so the buyer and seller receive the cash difference (credited or debited depending on the trade outcome) on the last day of the contract's life. Contracts are available quarterly in March, June, September, and December.

HOW DO INDEX FUTURES WORK - USING MULTIPLIERS?

In the case of the E-Mini S&P 500, the multiplier is $50 times the current value of the S&P 500. For example, if the S&P is trading at 5000, the total value per contract is $250,000. This, in essence, gives the trader the ability to hold a contract worth $250,000 with an initial margin with some brokers as low as $500 on an E-Mini trading at 5000.

Now, if we consider the volatility and liquidity within the Index Futures Market, we can see why it's become such an attractive market for speculators, retail traders, and institutional investors alike. Like the Nasdaq and Dow Jones, it's traded around the clock with electronic trading hours. Where stock options and shares are tradable during regular trading hours, index futures allow for virtually 24-hour trading. Woopa! Specifically, between Sunday 6 pm - Friday 5 pm, there is a daily maintenance break between 5 pm and 6 pm during the week. (Eastern Time) or UTC on your charts.

WHAT ARE THE BENEFITS OF TRADING INDEX FUTURES?

Let's start with the obvious - Leverage, Risk Management and Hedging.

Due to the levels of cash required to invest in individual stocks, futures provide an investor with the power of leverage. They can spend less to make more theoretically. Other benefits include risk management and hedging. Large investment funds or, indeed, some speculators may hold a large stock portfolio. If the market declines, they may be inclined to sell the futures contract for the specific index to mitigate any losses vs selling their portfolio for a loss. By selling futures contracts, they would make profits, offsetting the losses in their stock holdings. With hedging, a fund manager or portfolio manager may want to protect against "probable losses", so they may buy futures contracts in a falling market. This approach would diminish overall profits but mitigate share price fluctuations.

Let's now consider how a trader makes money using the S&P Futures Index (Ticker: ES) as an example.

WORKED EXAMPLE – E-MINI S&P 500 FUTURES

Tick value is the amount of money made or lost per incremental change. Today, it moves in 0.25-point increments, with each increment equating to $12.50 per contract. A full-point move would, therefore, be $50. Another way of looking at it is for every $1 change on the S&P, you'd set to gain c$50.

Let's consider ESM2024, which, for clarity, would be the June contract, trading at 5000, and you decide to buy 1 contract expecting it to break out to 5020. Here's how that would look in dollars and cents.

Assuming you bought 1 contract at 5000 with a stop loss at 4995, your risk would be $250 (50 x 5 points).

With a limit sell set at 5020, the anticipated profit would be $1000 (50 x 20 points), holding a risk to reward of 1/4, the lowest Risk to Reward I'll consider on any trade for clarity.

In short, if a speculator buys a futures contract and the underlying asset goes up, so will the futures contract, and therefore, a profit is made. Equally, if the speculator sells the futures derivative and the underlying goes down, the speculator profits. Of course, if the speculator buys and the underlying asset goes down, the investor would be set to lose money. They can, of course, top up their position by adding into a losing position should they anticipate future growth (when bullish) or close out the position to minimise losses. However, as mentioned before, futures trading is extremely volatile. If it is not appropriately managed, your broker will request a margin call. I.e., your broker will want more money from you to maintain the position.

Nasdaq 100 (Ticker: NQ) is another popular example so let's break down an example.

NQ has a tick size of 0.25 with each increment equating to $5. So, for every 1 point move you'd set to either gain, or lose $20 depending on direction.

Let's look at the formula again;

(Settlement price − Initial Price) x Contract Size x Number of Contracts

Or, in numbers; Let's assume you bought 2 contracts at $18,000 expecting price to rally up to $18,100. You would calculate your profit as follows.

($18,100 − $18,000) x $20 x 2 contracts = $4,000

Reverse engineering it by looking at tick values we can do the following.

$100 / 0.25 tick size = 400 ticks

Now, multiply the tick increments by the tick value.

400 ticks x $5 = $2,000

Simply multiply this figure by the number of contracts.

$2000 x 2 contracts = $4,000

Now if you think this is tricky just stay with it, the more you practice it the easier it becomes, hence why I've left pages in the back for you to have fun with. If it helps at all, I received a C in Math at School. Business Studies, A. But Math, Meh! If only my teacher could see me now.

E-MINI AND MICRO CONTRACTS

A brief history here, forgive me, but it is worth knowing. In 1982, CME introduced the standard-sized stock index futures contract, based on the S&P 500, and traded under the ticker SP on the CME's Globex platform. Priced at $250 times the value of the S&P 500, this contract was primarily targeted at large institutional investors for hedging or speculation purposes. To put that into perspective, one contract was a multiple of 250 times the value of the S&P! So, if the S&P was trading at 2000 back then, the contract was worth $500,000. Today, that same contract would be worth over $1 Million.

However, its substantial value made it inaccessible to many smaller traders who were interested if it were more affordable. Responding to this demand, CME launched the first E-mini contract in September 1997, which was also based on the S&P 500 but with a value one-fifth that of the full-sized contract. While serving the same functions of hedging and speculation, the E-mini made participation more accessible to smaller investors, broadening the market landscape.

Interestingly, given the sheer accessibility now for both speculators and institutional investors and the ability to manage the same positions with a more manageable contract size, the CME delisted the original standard full-sized contract in September 2021 as interest waned.

What you need to know is that one E-Mini has a multiplier of 50 times the S&P.

In a nutshell: Tick Increments 0.25 at $12.50 per tick with 1 full point at $50. An E-mini contract provides the ability to leverage 50 times the current S&P value.

It doesn't stop here, though. For those seeking an even lower entry point, CME launched the Micro E-minis, often referred to as the Micros, representing 1\10th the size of the now defunct original contract. Again, it is based on the same underlying but now with a multiplier of $5.

In a nutshell: Tick Increments 0.25 at $1.25 per tick with 1 full point $5. A micro E-Mini contract provides the ability to leverage 5 times the current

S&P value. If you have a tiny amount of capital to deploy, you may want to consider the Micro E-Mini S&P500.

Both E-Mini and Micro E-Minis can be found across asset classes, some of which are noted below. Still, for Index futures, an E-Mini index futures is 1\5th the original contract size. A Micro E-Mini is 1\10th the size of a standard contract. Within the Index Futures asset class, they can be utilised on the S&P 500, Nasdaq 100, Dow Jones Industrial, and Russell 2000, providing even more traders access to the major index futures markets. I have broken some of those down for you below:

E-MINI & MICRO'S LIST

Here is a list across asset classes for Minis and Micros. For a complete list, check TradingView.

ES1! - E-Mini S&P Index Futures

MES1! - Micro E-Mini S&P Index Futures

NQ1! - E- Mini Nasdaq-100 Futures

MNQ1! - Micro E-Mini Nasdaq 100 Futures

YMQ1! - E-Mini Dow Futures

MYMQ1! - Micro E-Mini Dow Jones Futures

CL1! - Crude Oil Futures

MCL1! - Micro Crude Oil Futures

NG1! - Henry Hub Natural Gas Futures

MNG1! - Micro Henry Hub

BTC1! - Bitcoin Futures

MBT1! - Micro Bitcoin Futures

GC1! - Gold Futures

MGC1! - Micro Gold futures

Below, I'll break down some of the most popular index futures available in more detail:

INDEX FUTURES TRADING SPECIFICATIONS

1 - Nasdaq E-Mini Index Futures

The Nasdaq 100 Futures represent a derivative financial instrument based on the Nasdaq 100 Index.

Symbol: NQ (also known as NQM24 for the June 2024 contract)

Current Price: $17,526.50 (as of the last close upon writing)

Contract Size: $20 per point

Settlement Type: Cash settlement

Tick Size: 0.25

Tick Value: $5

Base Symbol: NQ

Point Value: 1 point = $20

2 - Nasdaq Micro E-Mini Index Futures

The Micro E-mini Nasdaq-100 futures (symbol: MNQ) is smaller-sized versions of the E-mini contracts.

Symbol: MNQ (also known as MNQM24 for the June 2024 contract)

Current Price: $17,526.50 (as of the last close upon writing)

Contract Size: $2 per point

Settlement Type: Cash settlement

Tick Size: 0.25

Tick Value: $.50

Base Symbol: MNQ

Point Value: 1 point = $2

3 - S&P500 E-Mini Futures

The S&P 500 E-mini Futures is a futures contract based on the S&P 500 index.

Symbol: ES (also known as ESM24 for the June 2024 contract)

Current Price: $5,076.75 (as of the last close upon writing)

Contract Size: $50 per point

Settlement Type: Cash settlement

Tick Size: 0.25

Tick Value: $12.50

Base Symbol: ES

Point Value: 1 point = $50

4 - S&P 500 Micro E-Mini Futures

The Micro E-mini S&P 500 futures (symbol: MES) offer smaller-sized versions of the E-mini contracts.

Symbol: MES (also known as MESM24 for the June 2024 contract)

Current Price: $5,076.75 (as of the last close upon writing)

Contract Size: $5 per point

Settlement Type: Cash settlement

Tick Size: 0.25

Tick Value: $1.25

Base Symbol: MES

Point Value: 1 point = $5

5 - Dow Jones Industrial Average (DJIA) E-Mini Futures

The Dow Jones Industrial Average (DJIA) E-mini Futures represent a futures contract based on the Dow Jones Industrial Average index.

Symbol: YM (also known as YMM24 for the June 2024 contract)

Current Price: $37,742.00 (as of the last close upon writing)

Contract Size: $5 per point

Settlement Type: Cash settlement

Tick Size: 1

Tick Value: $5

Base Symbol: YM

Point Value: 1 point = $5

6 - Dow Jones Industrial Average (DJIA) Micro E-Mini Futures

Micro E-mini Dow Jones futures are electronically traded futures contracts based on the Dow Jones Industrial Average (DJIA) index.

Symbol: MYM (also known as YMM24 for the June 2024 contract)

Current Price: $37,742.00 (as of the last close upon writing)

Contract Size: $0.50 per point (one-tenth the size of the standard E-mini Dow Jones futures)

Settlement Type: Cash settlement

Minimum Tick: 1.00 index point

Base Symbol: MYM

Point Value: $0.50

7 - E-mini Russell 2000 Index Futures

The E-mini Russell 2000 Index Futures tracks the performance of the Russell 2000 index, which consists of the 2,000 largest small-cap companies on the Russell 3000 Index.

Symbol: RTY (also known as RTYM2024 for the June 2024 contract)

Current Price: $37,742.00 (as of the last close upon writing)

Contract Size: $50 per point

Settlement Type: Cash settlement

Minimum Tick: .10 index point

Tick Size: $5

Base Symbol: RTY

Point Value: 1 Point = $50

THE WORLD OF PROPRIETARY FIRMS

So you may be thinking, well, all this is great, but I don't have the capital required upfront to cover either an initial or intraday margin. Well, fear not, as there is currently an emerging sector that caters to this investor. This sector is called Proprietary Firms, more commonly known as prop firms. Now, let's cut to the chase. Proprietary firms were initially born to cater to already experienced traders who could provide a proven track record that would essentially allow them to work for the firm and receive a percentage of returns. However, this has evolved. Once a barrier to entry, no more! You now no longer need to show three years of trading accounts to apply for a proprietary firm job. With options to choose from that are vast and seemingly never-ending, with new companies popping up every week, always make sure to carry out your own due diligence before deciding to engage with any firm, if at all. However, from personal experience, there are great firms to trade with if you look deep enough and spend time reviewing them. One I would personally recommend is TopStep should you be considering Index Futures or Commodities, a highly reputable firm that I still use to this day. Why? Because they have tons of great features, one being there is no upward cap on the amount that can be made over a certain period of time and another being their thoughtfully, newly released online platform that is integrated into Trading View. Of course there are other great features too, but for me, those are the ones that stand out. Should you wish to find out more you can find their information on the very last page of the book, along with a links on how you can learn and trade along with me live each day to help you on your journey.

WHY AND HOW DOES IT WORK?

Traditionally, a prop firm trader would trade using a strict set of protocols, closely monitored by the firm, and for good reason too, as the trader would be utilising the firm's actual money to trade the markets. However, this has evolved into allowing anyone with a basic understanding of the markets to trade synthetic money with no barrier to entry in return for real money profit splits once certain criteria have been met and achieved.

There is a catch, however, of course there is! In order to trade this synthetic money, you must pass an evaluation. Evaluations vary depending on which proprietary firms you use, but a typical account size is $50,000, and you are required to make $53,000 to pass the evaluation. On route to passing, you're required to navigate a plethora of rules. These typically include not hitting a max drawdown figure, typically 5% below the initial account size figure, and trailing drawdowns where your max drawdown trails behind your account balance until you reach your required profit target to pass. There are others, too, such as minimum trading days and consistency rules.

Once passed, you will be rewarded with a funded account of the same size. Here, the same rules apply, but once you reach your profit targets, you are able to withdraw funds based on the profits made. Again, there are various rules depending on which firm you use, but the principles are the same. Show consistent trading across a period of time, and you can request a payout. Usually, the first $25,000 is %100 yours. Beyond this level, the splits are, on average, 90/10 in the trader's favour. Payouts are made into your bank account and can usually be requested between two and four times a month - depending on which proprietary firm you choose. Now, once you have traded for an extended period and shown consistency, constantly withdrawing funds, they may reach out to you to trade with Live (Real Money). Up until this point, however, whether you are trading an evaluation or your newly acquired funded account, it's all synthetic.

Disclaimer alert: It should be said with the ever-competing nature of gaining your business, payout times and rules are ever-changing. So always ensure you carry out your own due diligence before deciding which proprietary firm to use, if at all.

So, X - If I do decide to go with a proprietary firm, what's the catch? Well, you have to pay to take an evaluation account, and once passed and approved, you have to pay again to gain access to your funded account. How else do you think they can afford the payouts?

Now, it'd be remiss of me not to raise the pitfalls, as often with new traders, here lies the problem. The relatively low cost to take an evaluation (often between $50 and $200) for a $50,000 account - means that many new aspiring traders come into the market with a flippant mindset seeking immediate riches! We've all heard this one before, right?

Once upon a time, someone would save $3000 or so to begin trading directly in the market. Now, that same amount is lost in minor incremental cuts via paying for Evaluation accounts with proprietary firms as they blow account after account, sometimes passing, spending even more money, only to blow that account, ultimately quitting before ever receiving a payout. There are ways to trade Proprietary firms and there are absolutely ways you should not trade them. One of the reasons behind Red Pill Trading, the trading community I set up in 2023, was to help people navigate this journey successfully. Something we're proud to say has worked with hundreds of traders achieving funded status and or receiving payouts since the start of 2023. I'll share some of those tips with you below, but first, let's look at the pros and cons of Proprietary Firms.

PROS AND CONS OF PROPRIETARY FIRMS

Pros Of Proprietary Firms:

- Leverage
- Access to the Futures Markets with limited initial capital
- Low barrier to entry
- Wide choice of firms to use
- Copy Trading Facility - (Ability to trade multiple accounts simultaneously)

Cons Of Proprietary Firms:

- Low Barrier to entry can lead to addiction similar to a gambling addiction
- Rules for passing are hard to navigate for new traders
- Lack of regulation
- No guarantee they will be around forever

How To Trade Proprietary Firms Correctly (Based on a $50,000 Account)

Before I lay some tips out below, know that I stick to my poisons. I.e., I predominantly trade Index Futures and Commodities. If you happen to trade Forex (which I do not), just apply the same governing rules.

Governing Rules:

- Pass your evaluation taking trades with a minimum 1`4 Risk to Reward
- Seek to make $500 per day MAX
- Only use 2 contracts maximum
- Once you hit your Profit Target for the day - Stop trading
- Set MAX loss rules - $300 per day
- Trading ES then seek trades with 2 cons for 5 points / NQ Seek 2 cons 1 x 10 points 1 x 15 fixed.

Do this for a week with no red days, and you pass your evaluation!

FINAL WORDS

So, there we have it; we have come to the end of this journey together, folks. You now have a broader understanding of the futures markets and the asset classes therein. You're now better equipped to make more informed decisions on whether trading futures is for you with, I hope, even more clarity.

As shown, the opportunities and assets available are vast so spend time on each asset class until you find one that resonates with you. If you, as the trader can apply time and patience to the markets, futures provide a great vehicle for trading the financial markets and reaching your financial goals and aspirations. So, if this book has helped you tip the scales towards trading futures, my advice to you would be; Go get it!

For all those inside Red Pill Trading who have read this book. A BOSH! Know that I have immense respect for each and every one of you, your work ethic and success stories continue to inspire me every day.

YouTube and X readers (Formerly Twitter), thank you for being part of the journey so far. Your trust in me will continue to be matched with valuable content that will aid your development.

For those still struggling, keep pushing. Trading is immensely difficult. On average, 90% fail and quit in the first year so let's be clear: Success stories are found in the setbacks! Every setback is an opportunity to learn, grow and iterate. With trading, you will hit setbacks, trust me! Success is found in working through to the other side time after time and never giving up. There is, of course, a host of free content on my YouTube channel, website, or Twitter feed, should you wish to sharpen your approach in any way.

Equally, if you ever want to reach out and ask me a question, please do. My aspirations are simple: to help as many people achieve financial freedom as possible. If I can help you in any way shape, or form, of course I will do. You can reach me at:

contactredpilltrading@gmail.com

or via:

www.redpill-trading.com

For a step-by-step guide on how to get started in the futures markets with me by your side, simply head to the last pages of the book.

My final words are this.

Genuinely focus on simply getting 1% better each and every and dial in on the process. Forget monetary gain and Lamborghini's for now. Perfect processes and money follows. With trading it can be tempting to focus only on the technical, but psychology is as important if not more. So, ensure you develop both parts equally. In trading that means developing your technical trading skills just as much as developing your ability to control emotions. Focus on the process and the rewards follow. Simple.

If this book represents your very first 1%, drop a comment on YouTube or X, saying "1%", so I know we're on the same level.

Stay safe and stay blessed.

TRADING FUTURES

GLOSSARY

Agriculture Futures - The classification of a combination of Asset classes. These include soft, grains, and meat futures.

Blue Chip Companies - Large, well-established corporations known for their track record of stable earnings, strong financials, and overall standing within their industries. They often lead their sectors and are widely regarded as some of the most dependable and financially secure investments in the stock market. Most notable is these companies are distinguished by their significant market capitalisation.

Bonds - Bonds represent debt securities issued by governments or corporations to generate capital. When an investor purchases a bond, they effectively loan money to the issuer, receiving periodic interest payments with the repayment of the principal amount upon maturity.

Bull Market - Linked with economic expansion, robust corporate earnings growth, and optimistic investor sentiment. In a bull market, asset prices, such as stocks, bonds, or commodities, generally trend upward.

Bear Market - Associated with economic contraction, sluggish corporate earnings, and pessimistic investor sentiment. In a bear market, asset prices, such as stocks, bonds, or commodities, typically trend downward.

Chicago Board of Trade (CBOT) - Refer to CME Group.

Contract Value Calculation - The futures multiplier is multiplied by the price of the underlying asset to calculate the total value of the futures contract. For example, with the E-Mini S&P 500 Contract, the multiplier is 50. So, if the underlying asset (S&P500) is trading at 5000, then the contract's value is worth $250,000 (5000 x 50).

CAC 40 - A stock market index representing the 40 largest and most actively traded companies listed on Euronext Paris, the primary stock exchange in France. The index includes leading French companies from various sectors, including financial services, industrials, consumer goods, healthcare, technology, etc. L'Oreal is an example.

Currency Futures - Standardised exchange-traded financial contracts that obligate the buyer to purchase or the seller to sell a specified amount of a particular currency at a predetermined price, on a specified future date. Each currency futures contract represents a specific amount of the base currency in the pair, quoted in terms of the counter currency. E.g., if the price of a EUR/USD currency futures contract is 1.1100, it means that 1 euro is equivalent to 1.1100 US dollars. Some pairs include (EUR/USD, GBP/USD, USD/JPY).

CD'S - (Certificate of Deposits) Offered by banks and credit unions, CD's provide a fixed rate of interest on money deposited. Similar to how you would treat any bank account, albeit CD's are usually higher than the national average rate. Most are fixed, but there are variable rates, too. Note that you lock in that capital for a period of time, and the lengths can range depending on the account. This money can be accessed, but there are fees for doing so.

CTA's - A commodity trading advisor (CTA) is a professional advisor with expertise in trading commodities and derivative instruments. CTAs can manage investment accounts or trade futures on behalf of clients. CTA's can be either an individual or a company. In order to become a CTA, you need to register with the National Futures Association (NFA) and also pass a set of exams, known as the 3 series exams, often referred to as the National Commodity Futures Exam. Once passed, you can offer services as a CTA.

Contract Month Codes - Used after the Ticker and before the year to identify the current contract. Those codes are as follows. March: Code H / June: Code M / September: Code U / December:

Code Z. Example, ESM2024 for Month June with the S&P 500 E-Mini.

CME Group - The CME Group is one of the world's largest derivatives exchanges, offering a wide range of futures and options contracts across various asset classes, including equities, interest rates, currencies, commodities, and alternative investments such as derivative contracts as discussed in this book. They own other subsidiaries, including the Chicago Board of Trade (CBOT), the New York Mercantile Exchange (NYMEX), and the Commodity Exchange, Inc. (COMEX).

Commodities - Are tangible assets, i.e., you can touch and feel them. Examples of commodities include gold, oil, and agricultural products. These assets can be traded directly or through derivative contracts linked to their underlying value.

DAX - Predominantly a blue-chip stock market index that represents the 30 largest and most liquid companies listed on the Frankfurt Stock Exchange (Frankfurter Wertpapierbörse, FWB). It is probably the most widely followed benchmark for the German equity market and serves as a key indicator of Germany's economic and financial performance.

Day Trading - An investment strategy where traders buy and sell financial assets within the same trading day, aiming to profit from short-term price movements.

Dark Pools - Represent private electronic trading platforms where institutional investors, such as mutual funds, pension funds, and hedge funds, can execute large block trades anonymously. These allow investors to buy or sell large quantities of stocks, bonds, or other financial instruments without impacting the price or signalling their trading intentions to the broader market. There are issues with how this undermines transparency in the market, but they aren't going anywhere.

Debt Instruments - Debt instruments represent a contractual obligation by one party (the issuer) to repay borrowed funds to another party (the holder) at a future date, along with periodic interest payments. Examples include bonds, treasury bills, and certificates of deposit. In these examples, the issuer is the Government, and the holder is the Investor.

Derivatives - Derivatives are contracts based on an underlying asset, which can include stocks, bonds, commodities, currencies, interest rates, or market indices. Futures contracts are derivative contracts, which is discussed within this book. Options contracts also fall under the category of derivative contracts. The value of the derivative is directly influenced by changes in the value of the underlying asset.

Debt-Equity Ratios - Debt-to-equity ratio is a financial metric used to evaluate a company by comparing its total debt to its total equity, which indicates the proportion of a company's financing that is provided by creditors (debt) versus shareholders (equity). It's calculated as follows: Debt / Equity.

Dow Jones Industrial Average - The Dow Jones Industrial Average (DJIA), often referred to simply as the Dow Jones, is an Index that consists of 30 large, blue-chip companies, including companies from various sectors, including industrials, technology, consumer goods, healthcare, and finance. Trading the Dow Jones derivative futures contract is possible through ticker. YM.

E-Mini - Essentially, they have a smaller contract size than the Standard Contract (1/5th), making them more affordable for individual investors and traders. The smaller size allows investors to participate in futures markets with lower capital requirements and reduced risk exposure. They aren't applicable to all Futures contracts. However, some of the most notable ones are E-mini S&P 500, E-mini Nasdaq 100, commodities E-mini Crude Oil, E-mini Gold, and currencies E-mini Euro, E-mini Japanese Yen. For a full list of available E-Mini contracts, refer to your broker.

ETH - Represents the full days trading hours for that specific instrument. You can toggle between RTH and ETH on Trading view. Futures Contracts can be traded in ETH, which are hours after and before RTH.

Energy Futures - they are standardised financial contracts that allow investors to buy or sell specific quantities of energy commodities, such as crude oil, natural gas, heating oil, and gasoline. Each futures contract represents a standardised quantity of the underlying energy commodity, typically measured in barrels (for oil) or British thermal units (BTUs) (for natural gas). Energy futures prices are quoted in terms of the price per unit of the underlying energy commodity. For example, if the price of a crude oil futures contract is $60 per barrel, it means that one contract controls 1,000 barrels of crude oil at a price of $60 per barrel. Notional Value = $60,000.

Equity Instruments - Represent ownership interests in a company and typically entitle the holder to a share of the company's profits and voting rights. Common examples include stocks and shares.

ETF - Exchange-Traded Funds are investment funds that are traded on stock exchanges, much like individual stocks or derivative contracts. They are designed to track the performance of a specific index. In the case of the SPDR S&P 500 ETF Trust (SPY ETF), it tracks the performance of the S&P 500 Index.

FTSE 100 - Owned by FTSE Russell, the FTSE 100 represents the 100 largest companies listed on the London Stock Exchange (LSE) by market capitalisation.

Financial Futures - Financial futures are standardised contracts that obligate the buyer to purchase or the seller to sell a specific financial instrument, such as a stock index, interest rate, currency, or bond, at a predetermined price on a specified future date (settlement date). Financial futures are based on a wide range of underlying financial instruments, including stock market indices (e.g., S&P 500, Nasdaq 100), interest rates (e.g., 10-year Treasury note), currencies (e.g., euro, Japanese yen), and bonds (e.g., 30-year Treasury bond).

Futures Market - Known as the futures exchange or commodities exchange. A financial marketplace where traders buy and sell standardised contracts at a predetermined price for future settlement dates in either commodity or financial instruments.

Financial Futures Asset Class (Interest Bearing) - Are derivatives contracts associated with underlying assets that are interest-bearing instruments. On U.S. exchanges, these futures contracts encompass a range of maturities, with examples including the 30-year Treasury Bond and the 10-year Treasury Note, both traded on the Chicago Board of Trade (CBOT).

Financial Instruments - Refer to contracts or documents that represent a monetary value or provide a right to receive / deliver cash or another asset. Some of those include Stocks, Fixed income Securities, ETF'S, Derivatives, or commodities.

Foreign Exchange Instruments - These instruments facilitate the exchange of one currency for another at an agreed-upon exchange rate. They include currency pairs traded in the foreign exchange market, as well as currency derivatives such as currency futures and options.

Fundamental Analysis - A method for analysing a security (Such as stocks) by reviewing underlying factors which may affect the intrinsic value. Although the list can be extensive, the most common elements of analysis include. Financial statements, Business Model, Management Team, Industry Trends, Value proposition, and Investment Risk.

Grain Futures - Standardised contracts that provide investors with the ability to buy or sell specified quantities of the underlying asset. These include corn, wheat, soybean, and oats, to name a few. Institutions, farmers, or producers can use them to manage risk or to hedge against positions in their physical holdings. Speculators can use them simply to gain from movements on the underlying. Futures contracts work by a multiple of the underlying asset. For example, if Corn is trading at $2.50 per bushel and the contract controls 5000 bushels, 1 contract controls $12,500 worth of Corn.

Gap Up - Refers to a scenario in the financial markets where the stock price of a small-cap company experiences a significant increase in value at the opening of trading, resulting in a gap between the previous day's closing price and the new day's opening price.

Hard Commodity - Include examples such as mined metals in copper, gold, and silver, along with energy resources like crude oil and natural gas. Their distinction comes from the fact they are sourced from geological deposits awaiting extraction. I.e., Mines.

Hargreaves Lansdown - Leading financial services company based in the United Kingdom, offering investment management, advisory, and brokerage services to individual investors.

Hedge Funds - Represent a pool of private investors' money where their own in-house fund managers use this pooled money in a wide range of strategies, which include non-traditional assets, such as the futures markets. Their goal is to earn through those investments and subsequently providing above-average returns to those initial investors. Black Rock would be an example of a hedge fund.

Hedging - Hedging is a risk management strategy used by investors and businesses to reduce or offset the impact of adverse price movements in financial markets or commodity markets. It involves taking a position in a financial instrument or commodity opposite to an existing or anticipated exposure, with the aim of minimising potential losses from unfavourable price changes.

Hong Kong's Hang Seng - Hang Seng Index (HSI) is a stock market index comprising the largest and most liquid companies listed on the Hong Kong Stock Exchange and represents as a benchmark for the overall performance.

Index - Used to track the performance of a specific group of assets, such as stocks, bonds, or commodities. Indices serve as benchmarks or reference points for investors and analysts to assess the overall performance and trends of a particular market or sector. For Example, the S&P 500. Refer to the S&P 500.

Initial Margin - This represents the per-contract minimum amount stipulated by the exchange, which must be upheld in the account to retain a position overnight. Often referred to as overnight margin, it ensures that sufficient funds are available to cover potential overnight price movements.

Intraday Margin - This is the minimum account balance mandated by the broker to maintain a position of one contract (either long or short) during trading hours. It's also known as day trading margin.

Index Futures - Are standardised contracts that provide investors the ability to buy or sell specified quantities of the underlying asset. These include the S&P 500, Nasdaq 100, and the Dow Jones. Institutions can use them to manage risk or to hedge against positions in their physical holdings. Speculators can use them simply to gain from movements on the underlying. Futures contracts work by a multiple of the underlying asset. For example, if the S&P500 is trading at $5000 and the contract controls 50 times the Underlying, 1 contract controls $250,000 worth of the S&P500.

Interactive Brokers - Interactive Brokers (IBKR) is a well-established brokerage firm known for its advanced trading platforms, wide range of tradable assets, and competitive pricing. It caters to a range of traders and investors, from individuals to institutions, offering access to global financial markets.

Institutional Investment Funds - Institutional investment funds refer to pooled investment vehicles that manage funds on behalf of large institutions, such as pension funds, insurance companies, foundations, and sovereign wealth funds. These funds invest in various asset classes, including stocks, bonds, real estate, commodities, and alternative investments, with the goal of generating returns for their institutional clients.

Japan's Nikkei - Often referred to as the Nikkei, it comprises 225 of the largest and most actively traded companies listed on the Tokyo Stock Exchange (TSE), representing a range of sectors in the Japanese economy, including sectors such as technology, automotive, finance, industrials, and consumer goods. Toyota, for example.

Liquidation - Also known as offsetting, occurs when a long or short futures position is closed out by the broker due to insufficient intraday margin.

Margin - Futures margin refers to the essential funds held in a brokerage account to safeguard both the trader and the broker against potential losses in an open trade. Typically, it constitutes a smaller fraction of the contract value, ranging from 3% to 12% of the notional futures contract value. Notional value being the total value of the underlying contract.

Margin Call - A margin call is a notification issued by a broker to a trader when their maintenance margin falls below a certain threshold deemed safe. Upon receiving a margin call, the trader is required to deposit additional funds into their account to bolster the margin and prevent their futures contracts from being automatically liquidated, potentially incurring penalties.

Maintenance Margin - Excess margin, also referred to as maintenance margin, refers to the surplus equity in a brokerage account beyond the minimum margin requirements, which are often set by the brokerage.

Max Drawdown - Is the maximum amount you can lose in a portfolio before you lose that portfolio.

Metal Futures - Are standardised contracts that provide investors with the ability to buy or sell specified quantities of the underlying asset. These include gold, copper, silver, platinum and palladium. Institutions can use them to manage risk or to hedge against positions in their physical holdings. Speculators can use them simply to gain from movements on the underlying. Futures contracts work by a multiple of the underlying asset. For example, if Gold is trading at $2000 per troy ounce and the contract controls 100 troy ounces, 1 contract controls $200,000 worth of Gold.

Micro - An even smaller contract size than E-mini contract at 1/10th the size of the Standard Contract. The smaller size allows investors to participate in futures markets with lower capital requirements and reduced risk exposure. They aren't applicable to all Futures contracts. Micros are available where E-Mini contracts; refer to E-Mini for some of the most notable. Refer to your broker for a full list.

Multiplier - The futures multiplier, also known as the contract multiplier or contract size, is a factor that determines the value of a single futures contract. It represents the amount of the underlying asset that the contract controls.

Nasdaq 100 - NASDAQ-100, often referred to as the NASDAQ, is a stock market index that tracks the performance of 100 of the largest non-financial companies listed on the NASDAQ stock exchange. It's well known for following technology companies.

NYSE - The largest equities-based exchange in the world based in New York.

Nifty 50 - Is a benchmark Indian stock market index that represents the weighted average of 50 of the largest Indian companies listed on the National Stock Exchange.

Ninja Trader - A leading trading platform and brokerage provider used by active traders and investors to analyse markets, execute trades, and manage their portfolios. Known for its advanced charting capabilities, technical analysis tools, and customisable trading features.

Notional Contract Value - Is the total value of the contract. You calculate this by multiplying the spot price (underlying assets current price) by the multiple in the standardised contract. Crude Oil Notional Contract value = $90,000 ($90 underlying asset x 1000 standardised number of barrels).

Options Trading - A type of derivative trading that involves buying and selling options contracts, which give the holder the right, but not the obligation, to buy or sell a specific asset (such as stocks, commodities, or currencies) at a predetermined price (known as the strike price) within a specified period of time (until expiration).

Physical Futures - Physical futures entail the actual delivery or receiving of assets upon the expiration of the contract. For example, corn or Crude Oil.

Proprietary Firms - Proprietary trading firms, or prop firms, are companies that traditionally engage in trading assets with their own capital across various financial markets. These can include stocks, currencies, commodities, crypto-assets, and other financial instruments. These have evolved into providing a pathway for any trader, regardless of experience. Opportunities start by providing access for any trader to trade those very same assets. TopStep is an example of the modern-day Proprietary Firm.

Positional Trading - An investment strategy where traders hold positions in financial assets for an extended period, typically ranging from weeks to months or even years.

Quarterly Statements - Financial reports that are prepared and released by publicly traded companies on a quarterly basis, typically at the end of each fiscal quarter. These statements provide detailed information about the company's financial performance, including its revenues, expenses, profits, and cash flows, for the three-month period covered by the report.

RTH - Represents the time when the Stock Market is Open. Between 9.30 am to 4 pm Monday through Friday.

Soft Commodity - Fall under the agricultural products category, ranging from coffee and cocoa to grains like corn and wheat, as well as livestock such as lean hogs and feeder cattle. These commodities undergo a growth cycle that culminates in harvesting, typically followed by further processing.

SHFE - Shanghai Futures Exchange is China's exchange for commodity futures.

Soft Futures - Are standardised contracts that provide investors with the ability to buy or sell specified quantities of the underlying asset. These include cocoa, sugar, orange juice, and cotton, to name a few. Institutions, farmers, or producers can use them to manage risk or to hedge against positions in their physical holdings. Speculators can use them simply to gain from movements on the underlying. Futures contracts work by a multiple of the underlying asset. So, for example, if Cocoa is trading at $2000 per

M/Ton and the contract controls 10 M/Tons, 1 contract controls $20,000 worth of Cocoa.

Small Cap Stock - Refer to companies that have small market capitalisation. Refer to Market Capitalisation.

S&P 500 - S&P 500, often referred to simply as the S&P or the Standard & Poor's 500, is a market-capitalisation-weighted index of the 500 largest publicly traded companies listed on stock exchanges in the United States.

Settlement Day – The Settlement day in futures marks the end of a futures contract, where all obligations are finalised. It's the designated date for the ultimate exchange of funds and, if applicable, the physical delivery of the underlying asset between the contract's buyer and seller.

Standardisation - Refers to the process of establishing specifications, terms, and conditions for trading futures contracts on exchanges. Standardisation helps facilitate liquidity and transparency in the futures markets by providing a common framework for investors in all forms to buy and sell contracts based on specific underlying assets or commodities.

T-Bills - Treasury bills, often abbreviated as T-bills, are short-term debt securities issued by the U.S. government to finance its operations and manage short-term liquidity needs. The most common maturities are three months (13 weeks), six months (26 weeks), and one year (52 weeks). T-bills are considered one of the safest investments available as they are backed by the U.S. government. Treasury bills are zero-coupon securities, meaning they do not pay periodic interest like traditional bonds. Refer to T-Bonds. Instead, investors earn a return by purchasing T-bills at a discount to face value and receiving the full face value at maturity. The difference between the purchase price and the face value represents the investor's yield. T-bills are issued through regular auctions conducted by the U.S. Department of the Treasury. Investors submit competitive bids specifying the desired amount and price they are willing to pay for the T-bills. The Treasury sets the discount rate or yield based on the bids received, with the highest accepted bids receiving T-bills until the auction amount is filled.

T-Bonds - Treasury bonds, often referred to simply as T-bonds, are similar to T-Bills, but are long-term debt securities issued by the U.S. Department of the Treasury to finance government spending and manage long-term borrowing. Treasury bonds have longer maturities compared to Treasury bills, typically ranging from 10 to 30 years. Investors who purchase T-bonds receive interest payments, known as coupon payments, at regular intervals (usually semiannually) until the bond matures. The coupon rate is determined at the time of issuance and remains fixed for the life of the bond. This element is the difference between T-Bills and T-Bonds.

Treasury Notes - Also referred to as T-Notes, they are, in layman's terms, a smaller version of the T-Bond with terms ranging between 2-10 years. What's slightly different from T-Bonds is that they're available to investors in competitive and non-competitive bids. What this means is the investor can either accept whatever yield the government sets, or they can attempt to set the yield and see if it's accepted. Interest payments are paid biannually until the end of the term (Maturity). You can buy them from the government directly or through a brokerage, retirement, or traditional bank.

TOCOM - Tokyo Commodity Exchange is Japan's largest and one of Asia's most prominent commodity futures exchanges.

Trading View - A charting platform used by 60M+ traders and investors worldwide to spot and chart opportunities across global markets.

Trailing Drawdowns - Are drawdowns on an account that a proprietary firm will set, violating a trailing drawdown will cause a violation of the rules and will result in the investor losing his/her account. As you make profits, the trailing drawdown will move the same amount behind your balance until you meet the desired profit thresholds where the trailing threshold stops.

Ticker - Are symbols used to identify different financial instruments. Ticker (ES) would be how you search for the S&P500 E-Mini contract, for example. But the same can be used for individual stocks too, such as TSLA identifying TESLA.

Tick Size - Refers to the minimum price movement or increment at which the price of a security can change on an exchange, which varies depending on which security (Futures contract) you trade. Tick size is typically expressed as a fixed amount or percentage of the security's price. For example, a tick size of $0.05 means that the price can move in increments of 5 cents, while a tick size of $0.010 means that the price can move in increments of 10 cents. To calculate the value per Tick Change, simply multiply the tick size by the contract value. (Crude Oil - 0.01 per tick x 1000 US Barrels) = $10 per tick. To calculate profit / loss, multiply tick value by tick change. I.e., moved 150 ticks? (150tick x $10) = $1,500.

Warren Buffet – A renowned American investor, business magnate, and philanthropist. Chairman and CEO of Berkshire Hathaway, a multinational holding company headquartered in Omaha. Widely regarded as one of the most successful investors in history, he is known for his value investing approach and long-term perspective.

TRADING FUTURES

ACKNOWLEDGMENTS

Writing this book, in some ways similar to my trading journey, has been a real journey filled with challenges, inspiration, and growth!

First and foremost, I would like to express my deepest gratitude to my family, starting with my better half Rebecca, who has always been a brick in my life and for allowing me to stay up late into the early hours whilst bashing away on the keyboard! Your holiday is promised! My mother, too, for being a literary inspiration and sounding board as I progressed. Your love and belief in me has been my guiding light, and to my brother, for aiding with the overall design.

A massive heartfelt thanks to my friends and colleagues who have offered their truly valuable insights, feedback, and encouragement along the way. 1/5th not 1/4th! Little inside joke there. Your presence has enriched the content of this book without a shadow of a doubt.

I'm also indebted to the team for their professionalism, expertise, and dedication in bringing this book to life. Your guidance and collaboration has been invaluable. Pavel, you're a legend!

Lastly, I can't forget the numerous experts whose work has informed and inspired many of the ideas presented in this book and throughout the course of my trading life.

Finally, I would like to express appreciation to the readers who have embarked on this journey with me. Your curiosity, engagement, and support mean the world to me, and I hope that this book serves as a source of inspiration and insight.

Thank you from the bottom of my heart.

SOURCES

Crude Oil Tanker Image:
https://www.reuters.com/article/idUSKBN21Z2A1/

Futures Trading: What It Is And How To Get Started, Chris Davis

Asset Classes for Futures and Commodities Trading, Ilan Levy-Mayer

Trading Gold and Silver Futures Contracts, Nick Lioudis

Grow Your Finances in the Grain Markets, Hank King

Livestock Hedging using Futures or Options, Steven C Blank

Advanced Agriculture Marketing, Eric J. Balasco

Deep Dive into Commercial Meat Futures
https://www.cmegroup.com/education/courses/understanding-livestock-markets/buying-futures-for-protection-against-rising-livestock-prices.html

*I never wrote things down to remember;
I always wrote things down so I could forget.*

NOTES

TRADING FUTURES

NOTES

TRADING FUTURES

NOTES

NOTES

NOTES

NOTES

FUTURES

Trade along with me..

①

Join TopStep and choose Account

TOPSTEP

②

Join Red Pill Trading and learn to trade alongside a dedicated community and trade live with me daily

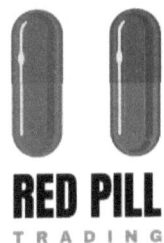

RED PILL
TRADING

FUTURES
Trade along with me..

③

Subscribe to Youtube for free content and Trade with me Live Tuesday & Thursdays

④

follow Twitter to stay up to date with current affairs

TradeX

① **TOPSTEP**

www.topstep.com

②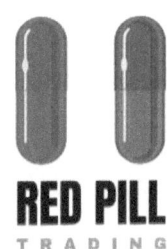
RED PILL
T R A D I N G

www.redpill-trading.com

③

www.youtube.com/@trade___X

④ X

www.x.com/Trade___X

www.ingramcontent.com/pod-product-compliance
Lightning Source LLC
Chambersburg PA
CBHW031625210526
45464CB00004B/1749